Eating The Oregon Way

A Guide to Cooking
With the Good Tastes of Oregon

by

Elsie Palmer *and* Jody Oeltjen

Illustrated by

Viki Bates

Published by
Berry Patch Press
3350 N.W. Luray Terrace
Portland, Oregon 97210

Copyright © 1982 by Elsie Palmer and Jody Oeltjen
Printed by ArtLine Printing Company, Inc.

Library of Congress Catalog Card Number: 82-73683

ISBN 0-9609912-0-4
2nd Printing, 1984
Printed in United States of America

$8.95

Table of Contents

About This Book . . .

Welcome to a taste tour of Oregon! Whether you want to enjoy shrimp, salmon or crab dipped from the sea, sun-ripened strawberries, raspberries, or blueberries fresh from the farm, or cheeses from the coast, in this book you will find recipes that include these and many other tastes of Oregon.

Eating the Oregon Way is much more than just a collection of our favorite recipes. It is an informal source of suggestions for obtaining and using the fantastic natural products available just a short drive from home. It can also be a guide for families who want to explore Oregon and experience it's uniqueness.

Today's household cooks are faced with the tremendous responsibility of serving foods that will maintain the healthy bodies and alert minds of their families. The recipes in this book are tailored to help lighten the burden by using foods that can be assembled ahead of time, or require a minimum of preparation and clean-up. We also recommend using foods that are in season because they taste best and cost less.

Eating the Oregon Way proves that tasty wholesome meals can be prepared and served even though time is short. Today's crowded schedules often mean "cooking on the run", but good planning and forethought will enable you to serve wholesome well-balanced meals with much more ease than you may think possible.

We are proud to offer you **Eating the Oregon Way.** We hope it will bring you enjoyment and confidence whether you are at home with your family or entertaining friends.

STIRRING ONCE,
STIRRING TWICE

Stirring Once, Stirring Twice

Soups

Stirring Once, Stirring Twice

Soups

When your family returns home on a dark, cold, rainy day, seeking the warmth and bright lights of the kitchen, there is really nothing quite like having a pot of soup simmering on the stove to greet them. The chilly wet days of our Oregon Fall and Winter will be brightened when you enjoy hot soup often.

In this section of the book you will find soups that are economical, nutritious, delicious, and versatile as either a first course or a main meal. We think you'll agree that you're always better off preparing your own soups.

Soup making is a delightfully simple pleasure. By using your own ingredients instead of the expensive, salty, chemical-laden packaged soup mixes you will be sure to save money and provide for your family a real nutritious first-class soup. Making your own soup stocks is easier than you may think. When made in quantities for the freezer it becomes a real convenience to use in many recipes.

Usually the makings of these soups are right in your kitchen. However, some of the best soups are created by improvising when a called-for ingredient is missing. The pioneers who travelled by covered wagon across the Oregon Trail often found it necessary to improvise. They brought with them cherished recipes, but soon new ones were created in log cabins and frontier homes by improvising with the foods that were available. We hope that you will try every soup and that some will become your "cherished recipes", too.

Italian Meatball Stew

As the snow season approaches many Oregonians look forward with great enthusiasm to Winter fun at Mount Hood. The choices for a fun day in the snow range from snowshoeing, cross-country skiing, tubing, downhill skiing to dogsledding. How lucky we are that we can drive to and from the mountain so conveniently and that we can breakfast at home, lunch on the mountain, and be back home for dinner. This stew is perfect to have cooking while you're enjoying the snow, and what a welcome smell to return to!

INGREDIENTS: *Serves 4 - 6*

1½	pounds lean ground beef	1	6 ounce can tomato paste
½	cup fine bread crumbs	1	cup water
2	eggs, beaten	1	cup homemade beef stock, fat skimmed
¼	cup milk	½	t crushed oregano
2	T Parmesan cheese	¾	t basil
¼	t garlic powder	1	cup frozen peas
	freshly ground pepper	1	cup frozen corn
2	carrots, cut in 1″ slices		

PREPARATION:

(a)   Combine beef, bread crumbs, eggs, milk, cheese, garlic powder, and pepper. Mix well and form into 1″ balls.

(b)   To cook in a crock pot, place carrots in bottom of pot, then meatballs. Combine tomato paste, water, beef stock, oregano, basil and pour over other ingredients. For top-of-the-stove cooking combine all ingredients in the pot and stir occasionally.

(c)   Cover and cook on low heat for 4 - 6 hours. Turn to high heat, add vegetables, cover and cook 15 - 20 minutes.

Salmon Corn Chowder

Winter Sunday night meals to us usually mean keeping work and preparation to a minimum. With the fire going it's easy to get up a good game of checkers or monopoly. Making this soup enables one player to take a quick time out and return with steaming bowls of soup on a tray so you hardly miss a move!

INGREDIENTS: *Serves 4*

1	16 ounce can pink salmon, drained and flaked
2	T butter or margarine
1	small onion, chopped
3	small potatoes, diced
1¾	cups milk
2	T unbleached white flour
1	cup frozen corn
	salt to taste
	freshly ground pepper
	fresh parsley, chopped

PREPARATION:

(a) Empty salmon into bowl and carefully go through it to remove bones, skin and dark meat. Reserve liquid.

(b) Melt butter in saucepan and saute onions until tender. Add potatoes. Add enough salmon liquid and water to make 1½ cups.

(c) Cover and simmer gently 20 minutes or until potatoes are tender.

(d) Stir flour into milk, and add it along with the salmon, corn, salt and pepper to potato mixture.

(e) Stir and cook the soup over medium heat until it thickens slightly. Ladle into hot bowls and top with parsley.

Jane and Eric's Lentil Soup

There is nothing like a hike in the Columbia River Gorge in the Fall. The Oeltjens had their first real hiking experience when introduced to this wonderful pastime by the Palmers. Seeing Punch Bowl Falls at the top of the trail is a rewarding experience. Your family will also feel rewarded if this soup is waiting at home in the crock pot upon returning from a day in the outdoors.

INGREDIENTS: *Serves 6 - 8*

3	T vegetable oil
1	large onion, chopped
1	clove garlic, minced
1	pound ground sausage
1	30 ounce can tomato sauce
2	carrots, chopped
2	stalks celery with leaves, chopped
2	cups lentils
3	T fresh parsley, chopped or 2 T dried parsley
3	cups water
2	T tamari (soy sauce)
	freshly ground pepper
1	t summer savory

PREPARATION:

(a)   Saute onion and garlic in the oil, then add sausage and cook until browned.

(b)   Stir in remaining ingredients and bring to a boil. Transfer to crock pot and let simmer for hours, adding hot water, if needed, for desired consistency.

Harvest Vegetable Soup

This is the perfect soup to serve on a night when everyone needs to dip from the "soup pot" at different times. It's a quick soup to prepare and it can simmer for hours. This soup commands a second serving—especially from children who usually don't care for many of the cooked vegetables.

INGREDIENTS: *Serves 6 - 8*

1	pound lean ground beef
1	medium onion, chopped
1	cup carrots, diced
1	cup celery, diced
1	1 pound 12 ounce can whole tomatoes
2	cups homemade beef stock, fat-skimmed
1	cup tomato juice
1	1¼ pound package frozen mixed vegetables
2	T long-grained brown rice
1	bay leaf, crushed
1	T Italian herb
1	t garlic powder
	salt to taste
	freshly ground pepper

PREPARATION:

(a) Brown meat in heavy soup pot. Drain if necessary. Add onions and cook one minute.

(b) Add all other ingredients and cook on high heat until soup comes to a good boil. Cover and simmer for 20 minutes or until ready to eat.

Cheese Topped Mexican Stew

This four-star stew is an example of what imaginative cooks can do with a bounty of fresh tomatoes and green peppers. The baking of this unique combination of the green chiles, meats, fresh vegetables, and Jack cheese is so good that we promise you compliments.

INGREDIENTS: *Serves 4 - 6*

1	pound beef stew meat, cubed		2	t cumin
1	pound pork, cubed		1	large green pepper, chopped
1	clove garlic, minced		2	4 ounce cans green chiles, diced
1/3	cup fresh parsley, chopped		1	cup dry red wine (or 2 T red wine
4	cups fresh tomatoes, diced			vinegar and water to make 1 cup)
1	t sugar		1	cup Monterey Jack cheese, shredded
1/4	t ground cloves			

PREPARATION

(a)   Brown meat, add seasonings, tomatoes, green pepper, chiles and wine.

(b)   Cover and simmer or bake at 350 degrees for four hours to reduce and thicken. Remove from heat.

(c)   Top with Jack cheese and place in oven for 2 - 3 minutes or until cheese is melted.

NOTE: This stew may be made ahead and frozen.

Homemade Tomato Soup

Round out your Saturday midday menu with a steaming mug of this easy to make soup.

INGREDIENTS: *Serves 4 -6*

2	t onion, finely chopped
2	T butter or margarine
2½	T unbleached white flour
	freshly ground pepper
3	cups tomato juice
3	cups cold milk
	chopped chives for garnish

PREPARATION:

(a) Saute onion in butter. Then add flour and pepper. Cook until smooth and bubbly, stirring constantly.

(b) Remove from heat and gradually stir in tomato juice. Bring to boil while stirring constantly. Boil about one minute.

(c) Stir hot tomato mixture gradually into *cold* milk. Heat rapidly to serving temperature.

(d) Serve topped with chopped chives.

Pioneer Sausage Corn Chowder

Jody's family loves to make homemade sausage once or twice a year. This chowder is one of their favorite ways to use some of the sausage. The first time she made this her husband, Ed, had three bowlsful! It's a hearty meal when served with crusty bread sticks and a raw vegetable plate.

INGREDIENTS: *Serves 6 - 8*

4	German sausages, broiled or grilled*	1	4 ounce can diced green chiles
1	large onion, chopped	1	2 ounce jar sliced pimientos, drained
1	large potato, peeled and diced	2	cups half-and-half or milk
1	cup water	1	t garlic powder
2	17 ounce cans cream style corn		freshly ground pepper

PREPARATION:

(a)   Slice sausage and saute with the onion. Cook until onion is limp.

(b)   Stir in the potato and water.

(c)   Cover, bring to boil, reduce heat, and simmer about 15 minutes or until potato is tender.

(d)   Stir in the corn, chiles, pimiento, half-and-half, and seasonings.

(e)   Heat uncovered, until it steams. Do not boil.

(f)   Ladle into soup bowls and enjoy!

*For homemade German sausages, see recipe on page 115.

Hearty Cheese and Salmon Soup

It's fun going to the Tillamook, Oregon area where you can drive through the peaceful country-side dotted with picturesque dairy farms. Nestled next to the coast, this area is lush with green pastures where cattle graze contentedly. Here you can find local cheese factories where you can view the cheese-making processes and sample some of the great tastes of Oregon. We hope you enjoy this taste of the cheddar cheese and salmon combination. It's a real winner!

INGREDIENTS: *Serves 4 - 6*

3	T butter or margarine
1	large onion, chopped
2	stalks celery, chopped
3	medium potatoes, diced
2	T unbleached white flour
3	cups milk
1	cup frozen peas
1	1 pound can salmon, drained and flaked
2	cups cheddar cheese, shredded

PREPARATION:

(a)   Melt butter in a heavy soup pot; add onion, celery, and potato. Saute until tender. Sprinkle flour over vegetables and cook until mixture is smooth.

(b)   Stir in milk and bring to a boil slowly, stirring constantly. Boil 1 minute while continuing to stir.

(c)   Add peas, salmon, cheese and cook until well heated.

Sheepherder's Camp Soup

This soup reminds Jody of driving through the rural mountain areas of Idaho where the sheep-herders would be herding their flocks to Winter pastures. Vicki Parkinson, from Boise, first introduced her to this hearty soup which is perfect for a crisp Fall night.

INGREDIENTS: *Serves 4 - 6*

1	cup pinto beans		1	15 ounce can tomato sauce
2	cloves garlic, minced		1	30 ounce can whole tomatoes
4	T apple cider vinegar		1	small head cabbage, shredded
½	pound bacon			water to barely cover soaked beans
1	onion, chopped			salt to taste
4	carrots, chopped			freshly ground pepper

PREPARATION:

(a)   Boil one cup pinto beans 2½ hours or soak overnight and boil 15 minutes.

(b)   Add garlic and vinegar

(c)   Fry the bacon and saute the onion. Drain.

(d)   Put all into the soup pot and add carrots, tomato sauce, tomatoes, salt and pepper.

(e)   After it has boiled one hour add cabbage.

(f)   Cook about 12 minutes or until cabbage is done.

Elsie's Easy Chili

Chili fans . . . this chili competes with the best of them in any chili contest. It's unbelievably easy.

INGREDIENTS: *Serves 4 - 6*

3	T vegetable oil
1	pound lean ground beef, or chili meat
2	large onions, chopped
2	large cloves garlic, minced
2	T chili powder
1	16 ounce can tomatoes
1	29 ounce can tomato sauce
2	cups cooked pinto or red beans
1	t crushed oregano
1	t cumin

PREPARATION:

(a) In a large, heavy pan heat the oil and cook onions and garlic until transparent. Add the meat and cook until well browned.

(b) Add all other ingredients and stir until well mixed.

(c) Simmer for 3 - 4 hours, stirring occasionally.

Thick and Creamy Chicken Soup

When the yard and fields are white and more snow is expected, plan this warm, tempting soup for dinner. You'll have a hard time surpassing this classic.

INGREDIENTS: *Serves 4 - 6*

4	T butter or margarine		2	cups cooked chicken, diced
3	carrots, chopped		½	cup milk
1	large onion, chopped		2	egg yolks
2	stalks celery, chopped		1	t poultry seasoning
3	small potatoes, chopped			salt to taste
½	cup unbleached white flour			freshly ground pepper
6	cups homemade chicken stock, fat-skimmed			

PREPARATION:

(a)   Melt the butter in a heavy soup pot. Add the vegetables and saute 3 to 5 minutes.

(b)   Blend in flour and stir over medium heat until smooth and bubbly.

(c)   Add chicken stock and seasonings; cover and simmer for 25 - 30 minutes.

(d)   Place half of vegetables and stock in the blender and blend until smooth, then return to soup pot.

(e)   Beat together milk and egg yolks and add to soup. Add chicken and heat thoroughly.

Old-Fashioned Beef Stew

This stew is good to make on a day when you are balancing the Christmas shopping, household errands, and carpools. It's ideal for serving a hungry family since the meat and vegetables compliment and health-balance each other.

INGREDIENTS: *Serves 4 - 6*

2	pounds beef chuck, cut into 1½″ cubes	⅛	t ground cloves
1	large onion, chopped		salt to taste
1	clove garlic, minced		freshly ground pepper
4	cups water	6	carrots, quartered
1	T lemon juice	4	stalks celery, sliced thick
1	t sugar	1	16 ounce can small white onions
1	T Worcestershire sauce	3	potatoes, diced
½	t paprika	½	cup water
1	bay leaf, crushed	¼	cup unbleached white flour

PREPARATION:

(a) Cut fat from meat and brown meat on all sides in Dutch oven. Don't hurry—this should take about 15 minutes. Add chopped onion and garlic, 4 cups water, and seasonings.

(b) Cook gently to make meat tender, about 2 hours. Do not boil.

(c) Add vegetables and cook another hour or until everything is tender.

(d) Shake together ½ cup cold water and ¼ cup flour to make thickening for gravy. Stir in flour mixture and cook until gravy thickens and boils a bit. Cook gently a few more minutes.

(e) Ladle into your serving tureen or serving bowls.

Corn Fish Chowder

What a special thrill it is to stand atop the storm-battered bridge at Depoe Bay and watch the fishing boats make their way through the rocky channel. We respect the fishermen who work so hard and make it possible for us to enjoy the many tastes from the sea.

INGREDIENTS: *Serves 4*

2	T butter or margarine
1	large onion, chopped
1	16 ounce can cream-style corn
1	cup milk
1	pound Oregon sole or cod
2	T chives, chopped
2	T diced green chiles

PREARATION:

(a)　In a soup pot melt butter and saute the onion.

(b)　Combine corn and milk in blender and blend only slightly, so that corn remains in small pieces.

(c)　Pour corn and milk combination into soup pot and add fish, chives, and chiles. Heat slowly for about 25 minutes, stirring often to prevent scorching.

(d)　Remove to heated soup bowls or tureen.

Ski Day Oven Stew

Imagine coming home exhausted after a terrific day of skiing on freshly powdered slopes. What joy to open the door and be greeted by the smell of beef stew cooking.

Put this stew in the oven for four to five hours and enjoy your ski time knowing that when you return dinner will be ready to serve.

INGREDIENTS: *Serves 4 - 6*

1	pound beef stew meat, cut into bite-size pieces
4	carrots, diced
4	potatoes, diced
1	10 ounce package frozen peas
2	T dried pepper flakes
2	stalks of celery, diced

1	28 ounce can whole tomatoes
1	cup water
½	t salt
½	t freshly ground pepper
1	onion, diced
2	cloves garlic, minced

PREPARATION:

(a) Put all ingredients into a roaster with a tight-fitting lid. Do not brown the meat. *(Everything cooks in its own juice, and even though it seems strange, the vegetables keep their firm texture.)*

(b) Place in a 275 degree oven and have a fun day!

Wintering in Vegetable Soup

While sitting by the fire working on this very book Elsie had a pot of this soup simmering in the kitchen, the smell enticing us so, that we could hardly wait for lunch. You might want to try this after the holidays as it is very low in calories, too.

INGREDIENTS: *Serves 4 - 6*

3	stalks celery, chopped
4	carrots, diced
1	large onion, diced
½	head cabbage, chopped
1	46 ounce can tomato juice
1	clove garlic, minced
2	cups homemade chicken stock, fat-skimmed
	freshly ground pepper

PREPARATION:

(a)   Combine all ingredients in the soup pot and simmer for two hours.

(b)   Serve and savor every bite!

Just Plain Good Soup

It's a cold day and you feel like eating soup. This is the one to make when you can't decide what to make and don't want to make a special trip to the store. It's made with very basic staple ingredients and is just plain good soup.

INGREDIENTS: *Serves 4 - 6*

3	T butter or margarine
3	carrots, chopped
1	large onion, chopped
2	stalks celery, chopped
2	cloves garlic, minced
3	medium potatoes, chopped
2	cups homemade chicken stock, fat-skimmed
1	16 ounce can tomatoes*
1	T fresh parsley, chopped
	freshly ground pepper

PREPARATION:

(a) In a heavy soup pot melt the butter; add carrots, onion, celery, and garlic. Saute until browned.

(b) Add remaining ingredients, cover and simmer for 1½ to 2 hours.**

*For a thicker soup, substitute tomato sauce for tomatoes.

**If time is at a premium when you are making this soup, increase heat and boil gently for 1 hour.

Thick Quick Minestrone

This man-style soup with full-bodied flavor is a variation of minestrone soup. It is low in cost, but really "sticks to your ribs".

INGREDIENTS: *Serves 6 - 8*

3	T olive oil
1	clove garlic, minced
1	large onion, chopped
2	carrots, diced
1	stalk broccoli, chopped
1	small zucchini, chopped
1	cup refried beans
1	10 ounce can tomato paste
1	quart homemade chicken stock *(or half stock and half water)*

½	cup short-grained brown rice
2	t tamari (soy sauce)
½	t rosemary
1	t basil
2	T fresh parsley, chopped
½	cup whole wheat macaroni
	Parmesan cheese for topping

PREPARATION:

(a)   Saute garlic, onion, carrots, broccoli and zucchini in olive oil for about 5 minutes.

(b)   Add all other ingredients, except macaroni and Parmesan cheese, and simmer for 40 to 50 minutes.

(c)   Add macaroni and cook 15 minutes longer.

(d)   Serve topped with Parmesan cheese.

Chicken and Broccoli Soup

When the calendar says it should be spring and yet chilly evenings make you want the warmth of a bowl of soup, this light, quick soup is the answer. You will also be pleasing any calorie counters in your family.

INGREDIENTS: *Serves 4*

3	cups homemade chicken stock, fat-skimmed
2	cups cooked chicken or turkey meat, diced
2	10 ounce packages broccoli, partly defrosted and cut up
1	cup dried minced onion
1	t dried thyme
2	bay leaves
¼	t garlic powder
2	cups low-fat milk
2	T cornstarch

PREPARATION:

(a)   Combine all ingredients except milk and cornstarch.

(b)   Simmer 10 minutes. Remove bay leaves.

(c)   Stir milk and cornstarch together until smooth, and then stir into simmering soup.

(d)   Cook and stir until bubbling.

FROM THE GARDEN

From the Garden

Salads

From the Garden

Salads

In Oregon we have the advantage of marvelous locally-grown fruits and vegetables — a luxury that not all parts of the country enjoy. Roadside stands, local produce markets and U-pick farms abound with freshly picked produce. Combine these with carefully chosen seasonings for truly magnificent tastes that are simple, elegant and fresh. A good salad fresh from the garden can turn a plain main dish into an exciting one, or it can become a meal in itself.

The perfect salad demands crisp, freshly washed fruits and vegetables, carefully selected and served in the most attractive fashion possible. We believe that the key to the perfect salad is "raw" — which makes for minimal loss of nutrients plus ease in preparation.

Probably no food you serve reveals more about you than your salads and their dressings. Here is an opportunity for you to be creative in the combination of ingredients, in the choice of colors and textures, and in the care you take to prepare and serve your salads.

By keeping on hand a wide variety of herbs, vinegars, salad oils, sprouts, cheeses for grating, seeds and other basic salad fixings, you can create your own interesting dressings, either subtle or dramatic.

Encourage your children to take one night a week to be responsible for the dinner salad. By working alongside them as they learn to clean, cut, core, pare, chop and serve, you will be helping them to develop a sense of pride and accomplishment, as well as encouraging them to develop new tastes.

Ham, Swiss Cheese and Potato Salad

For people living in the Portland area, the Columbia and Willamette Rivers offer water fun for sailboats, motor boats and canoes during hot summer days. Our families have enjoyed beaching the boat on the Columbia to picnic and watch the boat traffic. When a foreign cargo ship approached we jumped into the boat and sped out to get a closer view. We wanted to see the river pilot climb the outside ladder and board the ship to guide it into dock. We circled the ship several times then headed back for our picnic, returning the waves of the ship's crew. On your next river outing pack along this satisfying salad which will be sure to please your crew. For best taste, prepare it at least one day ahead.

INGREDIENTS: *Serves 4*

1½	pounds potatoes	¾	t salt
4½	T white wine (or 3½ t water and 1 T more of the vinegar)	1	t pepper
		½	cup vegetable oil
3	T white wine vinegar	¼	cup fresh parsley, chopped
¼	cup green onion, chopped	¾	cup cooked ham, finely chopped
3	T Dijon mustard	1	cup Swiss cheese, shredded

PREPARATION:

(a) Boil potatoes in jackets until tender. Drain and when cool enough to handle, peel and cut into ½-inch cubes.

(b) Combine wine, vinegar, onion, mustard, salt, pepper, oil and parsley in a jar. Shake and mix well.

(c) Add ham and Swiss cheese to the potatoes and pour two-thirds of the dressing over potato mixture. Mix until well blended.

(d) Cover and chill. Before serving stir and add desired amount of remaining dressing.

German Potato Salad

Spread the picnic cloth, unpack the loaded basket, and be ready to share the recipe for this tangy potato and bacon salad.

INGREDIENTS: *Serves 4 - 6*

4	medium potatoes, boiled in their jackets		2	t salt
4	slices bacon		¾	t celery seeds
⅔	cup chopped onion			freshly ground pepper
3	T flour		1	cup water
2	T sugar		½	cup vinegar

PREPARATION:

(a)   Cool boiled potatoes; then peel and slice thinly.

(b)   Fry bacon; drain on absorbent paper and crumble. Reserve small amount of bacon fat; saute the onion in the bacon fat until golden.

(c)   In the same skillet add the flour and seasonings to the onion and cook over low heat, stirring until smooth and bubbly. Remove from heat.

(d)   Stir in water and vinegar. Bring to boil, stirring constantly. Boil 1 minute.

(e)   Stir in potatoes and crumbled bacon carefully. Remove from heat. Cover. This can be served either hot or cold.

Oriental Salad

When apple blossoms appear and spring yard work makes a quick meal necessary, try this one. The crunchy goodness of this salad will make you want to serve it often.

INGREDIENTS: *Serves 4*

¾	cup Japanese rice wine vinegar
1	cup vegetable oil
¼	cup honey
½	t pepper
	salt to taste
1	head leaf lettuce, cleaned and torn
4	green onions, sliced
2	T sesame seeds, toasted 10 minutes at 300 degrees
2	T sliced almonds, toasted 10 minutes at 300 degrees
¾	cup fresh mushrooms, sliced
1	cup cooked chicken, diced
1½	cups fried oriental noodles, toasted according to package directions

PREPARATION:

(a) Mix together in a jar the vinegar, oil, honey, pepper and salt. Shake well and store in refrigerator. (This may be done ahead. This recipe makes enough for two salads.)

(b) Combine all other ingredients except the noodles. Add dressing and toss salad; then add noodles and again toss lightly.

NOTE: This salad is also a great accompaniment to a meal when prepared without the chicken.

Chinese Pea Pod Chicken

Go on a flavor adventure with this Chinese chicken salad. It's such a happy way to escape the kitchen and still maintain your reputation as a creative cook.

INGREDIENTS: *Serves 4*

Dressing:

½	cup toasted sesame seeds, toasted 10 minutes at 300 degrees		3	T lemon juice
½	cup vegetable oil		1½	T tamari (soy sauce)
4	cloves garlic, minced		1½	T white wine vinegar
			¼	t ground ginger

½	pound fresh Chinese pea pods		1	bunch fresh spinach, cleaned and torn into bite-size pieces
½	pound mung bean sprouts		¼	cup green onions, sliced
1½	cups julienne strips of cooked chicken (or turkey)			

PREPARATION:

(a)   Mix dressing ingredients together and refrigerate.

(b)   Remove ends and strings from fresh pea pods. Large pods may be cut in half if desired.

(c)   Combine in a bowl the pea pods and bean sprouts. Add meat and spinach; pour dressing over. Toss gently.

(d)   Top with sliced green onions.

Double Teriyaki Salad

The artistry, freshness and ease of this salad make it ideal for casual entertaining. When you find a good buy on lean steak marinate and freeze some for future use. When it's time for entertaining guests you'll be glad you did.

INGREDIENTS: *Serves 4*

1	pound lean steak (such as round or flank)
1/3	cup vegetable oil
1/8	cup tamari (soy sauce)
1/8	cup honey

1	T apple cider vinegar
1	T minced onion
1	clove garlic, minced
1/2	t ground ginger

Dressing:

1/2	cup vegetable oil
4	cloves garlic, minced
3	T lemon juice
1 1/2	T tamari (soy sauce)
1 1/2	T white wine vinegar
1/4	t ground ginger
1/3	cup sesame seeds, toasted for 10 minutes at 300 degrees

1	head leaf lettuce, washed and torn
2	cups fresh asparagus, cut into bite-size pieces
1 1/2	cups fresh broccoli, cut into bite-size pieces
1/2	cup water chestnuts, sliced
4	green onions, sliced

PREPARATION:

(a) Cut meat into bite-size pieces, about 1/8 inch thick. Mix the oil, soy sauce, honey, vinegar, onion, garlic and ginger and pour over the meat. Marinate for at least four hours.

(b) Mix dressing ingredients and refrigerate for about an hour before serving.

(c) Lift meat from marinade with a slotted spoon and spread on a jelly roll pan. Broil 4 inches from heat for 3 - 5 minutes.

(d) Combine in salad bowl lettuce, asparagus, broccoli, water chestnuts and onions. Add dressing and toss. Add the meat and again toss lightly.

Bengal Salad

Fresh Oregon crab is one of our favorite seafoods to use. This exotic salad uses crab and shrimp combined with the textures and flavors of crunchy fresh fruits, nuts and vegetables. Prepare the dressing at least twelve hours before serving so flavors can blend. We thank Sue Brown for sharing a recipe too good to leave out of this book.

INGREDIENTS: *Serves 4 - 6*

Dressing:

1	cup whipping cream	1½	T lemon juice
1	cup mayonnaise	¼	t garlic powder
½	cup sour cream	¼	t Worcestershire sauce
⅛	t curry powder		salt to taste

1	cup celery, finely chopped	6	lettuce leaves, shredded
¼	cup water chestnuts, drained and sliced	½	cup Dungeness crab meat
¼	cup pineapple chunks, well drained	2	T toasted, unsalted
1	orange, peeled and cut into bite-size pieces		sunflower seeds
½	cup baby shrimp	¼	cup shredded coconut

PREPARATION:

(a) Prepare dressing by whipping the cream until fluffy, but not stiff. Blend in mayonnaise and sour cream.

(b) Fold in all other ingredients. Cover and chill for at least twelve hours.

(c) Toss celery, water chestnuts, pineapple, orange pieces and shrimp together. Arrange these on a bed of shredded lettuce.

(d) Sprinkle the crab over the top and add the dressing.

(e) Top salad with sunflower seeds and coconut.

Salmon Salad

One of Oregon's most spectacular drives is through the scenic stretch of the Columbia River Gorge. Visiting Bonneville Dam gives one the opportunity to see the salmon migrating upriver, either at the outdoor fish ladders or through underwater viewing windows. Seeing the impressive salmon in its upstream struggle makes us appreciate Oregon in one more way.

INGREDIENTS: *Serves 4 -6*

2	cups cooked and flaked salmon (or 1 one-pound can, drained and flaked)
1/2	cup peas, cooked and chilled
1/2	cup celery, chopped
2	T sweet pickle relish
1	T lemon juice
1/2	small onion, chopped
3	hard-cooked eggs, chopped
2/3	cup mayonnaise
6	lettuce leaves, washed and patted dry

PREPARATION:

(a) Combine all ingredients except mayonnaise and chill thoroughly.

(b) Just before serving toss carefully with mayonnaise so that all ingredients are moistened.

(c) Serve on crisp lettuce garnished with tomato sections or wedges of fresh pears and apples.

Mexican Salsa Salad

This is an unusual salad to serve with a Mexican dinner. The colors are beautiful so serve it in a clear glass bowl to add a festive touch to your meal. To insure freshness combine all ingredients just before serving.

INGREDIENTS: *Serves 4 - 6*

3	large tomatoes, diced
1	large onion, diced
1	large green pepper, diced
3	stalks celery, diced
¾	cup mild red chili salsa
1½	cups cheddar cheese, grated

PREPARATION:

(a) Prepare vegetables and cheese and chill all ingredients.

(b) Before serving combine vegetables, salsa, and cheese. Stir well.

Taco Salad

The classic salad that's perfect for a Mexican potluck!

INGREDIENTS: *Serves 4*

½	pound lean ground beef
1	T chili powder
¼	t cayenne pepper
¼	t cumin
½	head salad bowl lettuce, washed and torn
½	head of head lettuce, washed and broken
1	8¾ ounce can kidney beans, rinsed and drained

1	cup cheddar cheese, shredded
2	small tomatoes, diced
4	green onions, diced
	Thousand Island dressing
1	cup nacho-flavored chips, crumbled

PREPARATION:

(a)   Brown the meat, drain and add the chili powder, cayenne pepper and cumin. Chill.

(b)   Prepare and combine lettuce, kidney beans, cheese, tomatoes and onions.

(c)   Add the seasoned meat and dressing. Mix well.

(d)   Top with nacho chips.

NOTE: Here are some tips to retain freshness and crispness when carrying this salad to a picnic or potluck. In a large salad bowl combine the seasoned/chilled meat, the lettuce, kidney beans, cheese and onions. Place diced tomatoes, dressing and crumbled chips in individual plastic bags or small containers. Lay these on top of the lettuce, to be tossed into the salad just before serving.

Tostada Salad

Children would enjoy the festive touch of a pinata hanging over the table when this quick and easy meal is served.

INGREDIENTS: *Serves 4*

2	cups refried beans
1	cup cheddar cheese, shredded
4	green onions, sliced
1	small head leaf lettuce, cleaned and torn
2	medium tomatoes, cut into bite-size sections
	Old-fashioned sour cream dressing
1	bag natural corn chips

PREPARATION:

(a)   Heat refried beans, either in microwave or on top of the stove.

(b)   On each plate spread one-fourth of the beans to about a 5-inch diameter.

(c)   Top with cheese, then onions, lettuce, tomatoes and desired amount of dressing. Garnish with corn chips.

Italian Tomato Slices

Outdoor markets and roadside stands around Portland make it possible for us to have an abundance of farm fresh tomatoes. This is a simple and unusual way to serve them, and the blend of the oregano and wine vinegar is delightful.

INGREDIENTS: *4 servings*

2   red-ripe tomatoes, sliced
      red wine vinegar
      crushed oregano

PREPARATION:

(a)   Wash and slice the tomatoes onto a large plate so slices do not overlap.

(b)   Sprinkle each slice with red wine vinegar and crushed oregano.

(c)   Serve chilled.

Crunchy Vegetable Chunks

One Fourth of July Elsie's friend, Carol Powers, brought these vegetables to a pre-fireworks picnic. Everyone enjoyed them as they sat on the beach of the Columbia River waiting for the fireworks to begin. We're sure you'll enjoy them, too.

INGREDIENTS: *Serves 6*

1	head of broccoli, broken into flowerets
1	head of cauliflower, broken into flowerets
6	large carrots, cut into 1″ pieces
2	large green peppers, cut into bite-size pieces
1	large onion, cut into bite-size pieces, or
1	16 ounce can small white onions
	low calorie Italian dressing

PREPARATION:

(a) Prepare all vegetables in sizes indicated above; place in a large covered bowl.

(b) Pour salad dressing over vegetables and toss so that all vegetables are coated. Refrigerate for several hours or overnight.

Marinated Onions

These marinated onions are a light, crunchy complement to a salad or sandwich. Be sure to try them in Rancher's Roast Beef Special and Grilled Turkey Deluxe.

INGREDIENTS:

½	cup cider vinegar
½	cup water
½	t honey

	salt to taste
1	large onion, thinly sliced and broken into rings

PREPARATION:

(a) Mix vinegar, water, honey and salt. Stir until honey is dissolved.

(b) Add onion, cover and marinate for at least three hours. They may be kept covered in the refrigerator for up to two weeks.

Marinated Cucumbers and Onions

INGREDIENTS:

½	cup cider vinegar
½	cup water
½	t honey
	salt to taste

1	medium cucumber, peeled and sliced
1	medium onion, thinly sliced and broken into rings

PREPARATION:

(a) Mix vinegar, water, honey and salt and stir until honey is dissolved.

(b) Add cucumber and onion, cover and marinate for at least three hours. They may be kept in the refrigerator for one or two days.

SERVING SUGGESTION:

Arrange salad greens on a chilled salad plate. Lift cucumbers and onions from marinade with slotted spoon and arrange on the greens; top with sour cream and sprinkle lightly with dill weed.

Marinated Mushrooms

Memorial Day weekend typically marks the beginning of the outdoor picnic season. These low-in-calorie mushrooms are perfect to tuck into holiday picnic baskets. They are very good!

INGREDIENTS: *Makes about 2 cups*

⅓	cup dry white wine (or 1½ T white wine vinegar & water to make ⅓ cup)
⅓	cup white wine vinegar
⅓	cup vegetable oil
¼	cup onion, finely chopped
2	T fresh parsley, chopped
1	clove garlic, minced
1	bay leaf, crushed
½	t salt
¼	t dried crushed thyme
	freshly ground pepper
20-25	fresh mushroom crowns, or 2 8-ounce cans mushroom crowns, drained

PREPARATION:

(a)   Combine all ingredients except mushrooms in a saucepan and bring to a boil.

(b)   Add mushrooms and simmer uncovered eight to ten minutes.

(c)   Ladle into a jar and refrigerate for several hours.

(d)   Strain marinade and return mushrooms to jar for carrying, or put into serving bowl for eating at home.

Crunchy Raw Vegetable Salad

This salad is so good! The combination of the fresh crunchy vegetables and the colorful appearance make it a welcome addition to a company dinner.

INGREDIENTS: *Serves 4*

Marinating dressing:

²/₃	cup tarragon vinegar		½	t salt
¼	cup vegetable oil		2	t sugar

1	head Chinese cabbage, cleaned and torn		1	cup raw broccoli flowerets, separated
1	green pepper, cut into bite-size pieces			
1	cucumber, sliced		½	cup bean sprouts
1	cup red cabbage, thinly sliced		¼	cup celery, diced
1	medium onion, diced			croutons
1	cup cauliflower flowerets, separated			
1	8¾ ounce can garbanzo beans, drained			

PREPARATION:

(a) Mix together all dressing ingredients.

(b) Prepare raw vegetables and marinate in the dressing at least one hour. Serve chilled with croutons on the top.

Spinach, Apple and Almond Toss

Here in Portland the first big event of the warm Spring season is the annual Rose Festival. All the busy festivities of parades, races, waterfront activities, visiting Naval ships, queen coronation, and rose viewing make quick, light meals a necessity. Warm weather and this spinach salad just naturally seem to go together.

INGREDIENTS: *Serves 6*

¼	cup vegetable oil		½	t prepared mustard
3	T white wine vinegar			salt to taste
1	t sugar			freshly ground pepper
5	slices bacon, browned, drained and crumbled		1	unpeeled red apple, cored and coarsely chopped
⅓	cup sliced almonds		3	green onions, thinly sliced
1	pound fresh spinach, cleaned and torn into bite-size pieces			

PREPARATION:

(a) Combine oil, vinegar, sugar, mustard, salt and pepper in a jar. Shake well and refrigerate.

(b) Cook bacon until brown and crisp. Drain and discard all but 1 t fat from skillet. Add almonds and heat until nuts are lightly toasted. Remove from heat.

(c) Combine spinach, apple, onion, bacon and almonds and toss lightly. Shake dressing and pour over salad. Toss again and serve.

Herbed Turkey and Spinach Salad

This spinach salad is highlighted with a marinated coriander dressing and uses cooked turkey. Making this will easily fit into your busy schedule, while doing your body a favor.

INGREDIENTS: *Serves 4*

³⁄₄	cup vegetable oil
6	T white wine vinegar
1¹⁄₂	t ground coriander
1¹⁄₂	t whole marjoram leaves
	freshly ground pepper
¹⁄₃	cup fresh mushrooms, chopped
1	small red onion, thinly sliced
2	cups cooked turkey breast, cut into thin strips
1	bunch spinach, washed and patted dry

PREPARATION:

(a) Combine oil, vinegar, coriander, marjoram, pepper, mushrooms and onion. Cover and refrigerate overnight or at least 3 hours.

(b) Just before serving add turkey pieces to the marinade.

(c) On each serving plate arrange one-fourth of the spinach leaves; then spoon one-fourth of the turkey mixture over each. Sprinkle more freshly ground pepper over the tops of each salad.

"The" Spinach Salad

The tangy mustard-flavored dressing is part of what sets this spinach salad apart from all the others. Serving it in a clear glass bowl makes it a real showpiece.

INGREDIENTS: *Serves 4*

Dressing:

1/3	cup red wine vinegar		1½	T prepared mustard
1	cup vegetable oil		1½	T sugar

1	large bunch spinach, cleaned and torn		2	hard-cooked eggs, chopped
2	stalks celery, chopped		5	large fresh mushrooms, sliced
1	small onion, diced		4	marinated artichoke hearts
1	cup mung bean sprouts		½	cup garlic croutons, crumbled
¼	cup water chestnuts, sliced			freshly ground pepper
4	slices bacon, cooked and crumbled			

PREPARATION:

(a) Mix dressing and chill.

(b) Combine spinach, celery, onions, bean sprouts, water chestnuts, bacon and eggs; toss again.

(c) Arrange mushrooms and artichoke hearts over the top. Then sprinkle crumbled croutons and freshly ground pepper over all.

Banana Creme Dressing for Fruit Kabobs

What fun Jane and Eric have dipping fruit into this banana creme dressing. It's perfect for a summer meal or as a snack that friends can enjoy together on the front step.

INGREDIENTS: *Serves 4 - 6*

2	small ripe bananas, peeled and mashed
1	T brown sugar
1	T honey
½	cup whipping cream, whipped

Strawberries, bing cherries (whole with stems), grapes, chunks of honeydew, cantaloupe, fresh pineapple or other favorite fruit combinations.

PREPARATION:

(a)   Mix all dressing ingredients and chill well.

(b)   Make kabobs by skewering fruit, or arrange fruits on a platter and serve with fondue forks.

Berry Patch Freeze

When you start daydreaming of summer and those white blossoms on strawberry fields, bring summer flavor into your day with this cool salad.

INGREDIENTS: *Serves 6 - 8*

1	cup sour cream
½	T lemon juice
¼	cup sugar
1	8 ounce can crushed pineapple, drained
2	bananas, sliced
2½	cups frozen strawberries, partially thawed
1	cup walnuts, chopped (optional)

PREPARATION:

(a)   In a large bowl, mix sour cream, lemon juice and sugar until well blended.

(b)   Fold in fruits, berries and nuts.

(c)   Freeze in mold or serving bowl.

(d)   Let set at room temperature 20 - 30 minutes before serving.

Frozen Creamy Cherry Salad

Every summer we are amazed all over again at the perfectly shaped Bing cherries that grow so big and flavorful in the Northwest. This salad made with Bing cherries is great on a hot summer evening.

INGREDIENTS: *Serves 4*

1	cup sour cream
8	ounces Neufchatel cream cheese, softened
2	T honey
1	16 ounce can pineapple chunks, well drained
1	pound fresh Bing cherries, pitted
1/3	cup almonds, chopped (optional)

PREPARATION:

(a)   In a bowl beat together sour cream, cream cheese and honey until well blended.

(b)   Fold in pineapple, cherries and almonds.

(c)   Pour into a 4½ cup mold and freeze overnight or for 6 - 8 hours.

(d)   Remove from freezer about ½ hour before serving, then unmold onto serving plate.

BETWEEN THE SLICES

Between the Slices
Sandwiches

Between the Slices

Sandwiches

In the fast pace of today, often the only time for a busy family to be together is at the evening meal. People who live in Oregon have the unique opportunity to spend time enjoying forrested mountains, ocean beaches, high desert, rushing rivers and waterfalls. The contents of this chapter include sandwich ideas for times when your activities leave minimal time for cooking.

A first-class sandwich can easily become a quick, balanced meal. Whether it's dainty or Dagwood, served hot or cold, the use of fresh and natural fixings is essential. Here in Oregon that means fresh crab, shrimp, salmon, Tillamook cheeses, delicate salad sprouts and a large variety of greens, crunchy vegetables and other sandwich accompaniments.

Just as we choose carefully what goes between the slices, we also are careful to select top quality breads such as sourdough, dark rye and our homemade wheat breads. Well-made whole grain breads are darkly rich and crusty. They have true grain-rich tastes of their own that help build healthy bodies and strong minds.

The next time your meal plan reads "sandwiches", prepare an attractive arrangement of sandwich makings using baskets, bread boards and trays. Call your hungry eaters to join in the fun of each making sandwiches to his own liking.

West Coasters

You don't have to live near the ocean to enjoy this delicious grilled West Coast sandwich.

INGREDIENTS: *Serves 4*

8	slices pumpernickel, dark rye or sourdough bread
3	T butter or margarine, softened
1	12½ ounce can tuna (water packed), prepared as tuna salad
1	pound bacon, cooked and drained
1	large tomato, sliced
¼	pound cheddar, Provolone or Monterey Jack cheese, sliced

PREPARATION:

(a)   Butter each slice of bread on one side for grilling.

(b)   On unbuttered side of bread layer in this order: tuna, bacon, tomato, cheese, then top with other slice of bread.

(c)   Grill until crusty, cheese is melted, and sandwich is hot.

NOTE: Serving these sandwiches on paper-lined rattan plate holders, with a dill pickle, crunchy raw vegetables and fruit slices makes a fresh, colorful presentation for your family or friends.

Seven Layer Shrimp and Salad Sandwich

This elegant open-faced sandwich was served at a going-away luncheon for Jody when she moved from San Francisco to Portland. The pink shrimp, green sprouts, mustard-flavored egg salad, and dark, coarse texture of the bread atop a bed of fresh green lettuce create spectacular color contrasts.

INGREDIENTS: *Serves 6*

6	hard-cooked eggs		2	T sweet pickle relish
6	T mayonnaise			salt and pepper to taste
4	T prepared mustard			

6	large leaves of leaf lettuce, washed and patted dry		6	large slices tomato
			4	ounces alfalfa sprouts
1	loaf unsliced dark, coarse-textured bread (such as whole wheat or 7-grain)		6	ounces shrimp, fresh or frozen Thousand Island dressing

PREPARATION:

(a) Prepare mustard-flavored egg salad by mixing eggs, mayonnaise, mustard, relish, salt and pepper.

(b) Arrange one large lettuce leaf on each plate.

(c) Cut a fairly thick slice of bread for each sandwich and place on lettuce leaf; top with egg salad.

(d) Layer in order the tomato slice, alfalfa sprouts and shrimp. Top each sandwich with Thousand Island dressing.

Oregon Bay Shrimp Supreme

Creamy melted cheese and shrimp dipped fresh from the sea make perfect partners for this piping hot golden sandwich.

INGREDIENTS: *Serves 4*

8	slices sourdough bread
	butter or margarine
	tartar sauce
6	ounces shrimp, fresh or frozen
4	large slices cheddar cheese

PREPARATION:

(a)   Butter one side of each slice of bread for grilling.

(b)   On the inside of four slices of bread spread tartar sauce.

(c)   Cover each sandwich with one-fourth of the shrimp.

(d)   Place cheese slice on each sandwich and grill until golden brown and cheese has melted.

Rancher's Roast Beef Special
(with Marinated Onions)

When the weather is warm and appetites need tempting, make these unusual roast beef sandwiches for a delightful supper treat. The marinated onions are the key to the unqiueness of this sandwich, so it's worth the time it takes to marinate them.

INGREDIENTS: *Serves 4*

8	slices sourdough bread
	butter or margarine
8	slices cheddar cheese
	marinated onions *(see recipe page 38)*
½	pound roast beef, thinly sliced
	horseradish sauce *(see recipe below)*

PREPARATION:

(a)   Butter one side of each piece of sourdough bread for grilling.

(b)   On unbuttered side of bread arrange in this order: cheese, marinated onions, roast beef, horseradish sauce.

(c)   Grill until cheese is melted and sandwiches are golden brown.

Sherry's Horseradish Sauce

2 - 4	T prepared horseradish
½	cup green onion, thinly sliced
4	T dry mustard
¼	t salt
1	cup unflavored yogurt (or 1 cup sour cream and 1 T lemon juice)

In a small bowl, stir together all ingredients until well blended.

Marinated Steak Pocket Sandwich

When you can't tear the family away from the big game, heap all these "fixings" on a big tray and join them in front of the fire. Don't be surprised if the aroma of this meat sautéing beckons someone to the kitchen to help expedite preparation.

INGREDIENTS: *Serves 4*

½	cup dry red wine (or red wine vinegar)
2	T olive or vegetable oil
1	large clove garlic, minced
¾	t dried oregano, crushed
	freshly ground pepper

1 pound lean beef steak (such as sirloin or flank), about ⅛" thick and about 2" long (cut against the grain)

6 - 8 pocket bread
3 cups lettuce, thinly sliced
2 cups tomatoes, peeled and diced
2 cups cucumber, diced
1 - 2 cups sour cream dressing (we prefer Hain Old Fashioned dressing mix, made with sour cream and mayonnaise)

PREPARATION:

(a) Combine wine, oil, garlic, oregano and pepper. Cut steak into very thin strips and place in marinade. Let set for at least one hour at room temperature or several hours in the refrigerator. (You may let the meat marinate for a day or two in the refrigerator, or prepare large quantities and freeze in meal-size portions.)

(b) Lift meat from marinade with slotted spoon and sauté in butter over high heat.

(c) Let each person fill his own sandwich (or sandwiches)!

Oregon Grinder

Half the pleasure of this hot sandwich is in its wonderful name. It tasted so good after spending a hard working day getting firewood in, that it needs to be shared. Maybe it will become a week-end special at your home, too.

INGREDIENTS: *Serves 4 - 6*

6	sourdough hero rolls, heated
3	T butter or margarine, softened
2	cloves garlic, minced
1½	pounds round steak, cut into bite-size pieces
1	large green pepper, chopped
1	large onion, chopped
1	8 ounce can mushroom stems and pieces, drained
2	tomatoes, diced
6	slices Provolone or Monterey Jack cheese, cut into strips

PREPARATION:

(a)   In a large skillet melt butter; then sauté garlic and meat.

(b)   Add pepper, onion, mushrooms and tomatoes. Cook until hot.

(c)   While rolls are heating add strips of cheese to ingredients in skillet. Drain juices.

(d)   Fill rolls and enjoy!

Sausage Krauters

The small German community of Mount Angel, Oregon annually hosts an end-of-harvest celebration. Visiting the Oktoberfest inspired the Oeltjens to stage their own celebration complete with German polka music, sausage, sauerkraut, and friends. We hope that trying these krauters will inspire you to celebrate your own Oktoberfest, too.

INGREDIENTS: *Serves 4 - 6*

1½	pound jar sauerkraut
⅓	cup herbed salad dressing
2	T onion, finely diced
2	t caraway seed
6	German or homemade sausages *(See recipe page 115)*
6	sourdough or whole wheat sausage-size rolls

PREPARATION:

(a) Drain sauerkraut; add to it the salad dressing, onion and caraway seed. Refrigerate for an hour or as long as overnight.

(b) Grill or broil sausages.

(c) Serve in buns and top with sauerkraut relish.

Garden Sandwich

It may be that during summer's gardening and food-harvest days you can scarcely get enough time for cooking. That's when you need to set out a light, easily-prepared summer supper. Eating this sandwich should make you feel that you are really doing your tired body a favor.

INGREDIENTS: *Serves 4*

8	slices whole grain bread
1	3 ounce package cream cheese, softened
1	large green pepper, thinly sliced
1	large tomato, thinly sliced
4	large fresh mushrooms, thinly sliced
1	cucumber, thinly sliced
1	small red onion, thinly sliced
4	ounces alfalfa sprouts
	red wine vinegar
	whole oregano
	freshly ground pepper

PREPARATION:

(a)   Spread all slices of bread with cream cheese.

(b)   For each sandwich, on one slice of bread layer green pepper, tomato and mushrooms. On the other slice of bread layer cucumber, onion and alfalfa sprouts.

(c)   Sprinkle entire sandwich with vinegar, oregano and pepper.

NOTE: These sandwiches are very pretty served open-faced, but then can be eaten closed.

Hot Cheese and Chili Combo

This is a unique sandwich with an exciting flavor blend. Don't hesitate to serve it to guests for a quick spontaneous get together.

INGREDIENTS: *Serves 4*

8	slices sourdough bread
	butter or margarine
4	slices cheddar cheese
1	7 ounce can whole green chiles, rinsed and seeded
	mild taco sauce
1	4 ounce can sliced mushrooms
4	slices Monterey Jack cheese

PREPARATION:

(a)   Butter bread on one side for grilling.

(b)   On unbuttered side of bread layer in this order: one slice cheddar cheese, green chiles, taco sauce, mushrooms and Jack cheese.

(c)   Grill until cheese is melted and sandwich is golden brown.

Hot Crispy Cheese Heroes

You're sure to score points with your family when you serve these delicious hot sandwiches after the Saturday soccer game!

INGREDIENTS: *Serves 4 - 6*

¾	pound Italian cheeses (such as Provolone, Mozzarella or Monterey Jack)
	leaf lettuce, washed and torn
1	medium onion, chopped
3	medium tomatoes, sliced
	olive oil
	white wine vinegar
	whole oregano
6	hero (submarine) rolls

PREPARATION:

(a) Cut rolls so they lay open, then place each on a sheet of foil. Generously layer cheeses on both sides of roll. Place each piece of foil with open roll onto a baking sheet.

(b) Bake oven rolls with cheese in 400 degree over for 12 - 15 minutes, or until cheeses are melted and rolls are crisp.

(c) Top with vegetables and sprinkle with oil, vinegar, and oregano. Then close each and wrap immediately in the foil for ease in eating. Roll back foil as you eat.

Hasty Hots

All of us have busy seasons when time for making meals is short. The utter simplicity of these sandwiches makes it a favorite for everyone — especially the meal planner.

INGREDIENTS: *Serves 3 - 4*

3	English muffins, split and toasted
6	thin slices cooked ham
6	slices cheddar cheese
1	large tomato, sliced
4	T cream cheese
	Parsley or alfalfa sprouts for garnish

PREPARATION:

(a)   Place a slice of ham on each toasted muffin half, then top with cheddar cheese and tomato.

(b)   Stir or beat the softened cream cheese until fluffy. Spoon a heaping tablespoon on top of each sandwich.

(c)   Place sandwiches on a baking sheet and broil 3 to 5 minutes, or until cream cheese is browned. Serve hot, topped with parsley or alfalfa sprouts.

Sausage Sandwiches

While browsing through Portland's open air Saturday Market, you may be enticed by the aroma of the sausage sandwiches. Jody's dear Italian friend, Judi Cavaliere, taught her the traditional way to make this Italian classic. It's a great sandwich and we want to pass it on to you.

INGREDIENTS: *Serves 4 - 6*

6	sausages, such as Italian or homemade *(see recipe page 115)*
6	sausage-size rolls
2	cups spaghetti sauce
1	large green pepper, finely chopped
1	medium onion, finely chopped

PREPARATION:

(a)   Grill or broil sausages.

(b)   Heat rolls and spaghetti sauce.

(c)   Put sausage in hot roll and add onions and peppers. Cover with heated spaghetti sauce. Wrap each in foil for ease in eating and to keep sandwich warm.

Pizza Sandwich Loaf

Have all these ingredients ready when you go out for your "Fall Family Work-In-The-Yard Day". Then when you come in exhilarated and exhausted, your hard-earned meal will take just minutes to finish.

INGREDIENTS: *Serves 4 - 6*

1	loaf unsliced Italian or French bread
1	pound lean ground beef
2	T onion, minced
1	clove garlic, minced
2	T Italian herbs
1	6 ounce can tomato paste
1	8 ounce can sliced mushrooms, drained
2	T water
1	cup Monterey Jack cheese, shredded
1	green pepper, sliced into rings
2	tomatoes, sliced

PREPARATION:

(a)   In a large skillet brown the meat. Drain, then add onion and garlic and cook 2 - 3 minutes.

(b)   Stir in Italian herbs, tomato paste, mushrooms and water. Cook until heated through.

(c)   Spoon mixture over loaf of bread that has been sliced in half lengthwise. Sprinkle with cheese.

(d)   Broil until cheese is melted and sandwich is hot.

(e)   Garnish with green pepper rings and tomato slices laid on both halves of the bread.

Mozzarella Stuffed Meatball Sandwich

The melted cheese centers of these meatballs make these sandwiches a delight to your taste buds.

INGREDIENTS: *Serves 4*

1	pound lean ground beef	1	cup tomato sauce
1	small onion, chopped	1	4 ounce can mushroom stems
¼	cup whole wheat bread crumbs		and pieces, drained
	salt to taste	¾	t dried Italian seasoning
	freshly ground pepper	2	cloves garlic, minced
16	half-inch cubes Mozzarella cheese	4	Italian rolls, heated

PREPARATION:

(a) Combine first five ingredients in a bowl and mix well. Add 1 or 2 T milk if needed to hold together.

(b) Divide mixture into 16 portions. Place a cube of the cheese in the center of each portion and form into a meatball.

(c) Place the meatballs on a lightly oiled baking pan and bake at 350 degrees for 20 to 25 minutes or until well browned.

(d) While meatballs are cooking, combine tomato sauce, mushrooms, Italian seasoning and garlic in a sauce pan or skillet and simmer over medium heat for about 10 minutes. Add meatballs and simmer for about 5 minutes more.

(e) Spoon meatballs and sauce into split and heated Italian rolls.

Crusty Hot Poor Boy Loaf

On the evenings when your kids are rushing in three different directions — piano lessons, gymnastics, karate, soccer or football — the house cook can quickly put together this hot Poor Boy loaf between carpools. Team it with a hot mug of soup and you will receive cheers from your fans.

INGREDIENTS: *Serves 6*

1	loaf sourdough or French bread	12	sliced summer sausage *(see page 116)*
½	cup butter or margarine, softened	12	slices Mozzarella cheese
2	t Dijon mustard	1	large onion, sliced
1	T parsley flakes	1	green pepper, sliced
½	t garlic powder		

PREPARATION:

(a)   Slice bread in half-inch slices — slicing to, but not through the bottom crust.

(b)   Combine softened butter, mustard, parsley flakes and garlic powder.

(c)   Between every two slices brush both sides with butter-mustard mixture.

(d)   Layer buttered slices with sausage, cheese, onion and pepper.

(e)   Place loaf on a large sheet of aluminum foil and wrap foil around sides and end of loaf, but do not cover top.

(f)   Bake in preheated 350 degree oven for 20 - 25 minutes, or until heated through.

(g)   Serve on a large bread board garnished with alfalfa sprouts and tomato slices.

Cheesy Chive Turkey

You'll like what fresh chives from the garden do to the taste and appearance of this hot turkey sandwich. It's handy to make, especially if you keep leftover turkey slices in your freezer.

INGREDIENTS: *Serves 4*

8	slices sourdough bread
	butter or margarine
	mayonnaise for spreading
2	green onions, sliced
4	large slices Monterey Jack cheese
1	large tomato, sliced
4	large slices turkey breast
4	T chopped chives

PREPARATION:

(a)   Butter one side of each piece of bread for grilling.

(b)   Spread mayonnaise on unbuttered side of each slice of bread.

(c)   Layer one-fourth of the remaining ingredients on each sandwich in this order: onions, cheese, tomato, turkey and chives.

(d)   Grill until cheese melts and sandwich is toasted and hot.

Grilled Turkey Deluxe

This sandwich is very filling. With a crisp salad and some fresh fruit it will satisfy any hungry appetite. The time it takes to prepare and marinate the onions ahead is well worth your effort.

INGREDIENTS: *Serves 4*

8	slices sourdough or dark rye bread
3	ounces cream cheese, softened
4	large slices cooked turkey breast
	marinated onions *(see recipe on page 38)*
	butter or margarine

PREPARATION:

(a) Spread each slice of bread generously with cream cheese. Add sliced turkey breast and several rings of marinated onions.

(b) Butter the outside of the bread and grill until heated through and golden brown.

Teriyaki Tenderloin on a Bun

While these teriyaki kabobs are cooking, a quiet corner of the hot barbeque can be used to toast the accompanying crispy French rolls.

INGREDIENTS: *Serves 4*

1	pound beef tenderloin, cut in 1″ cubes
2	medium onions, quartered for skewering
1	large green pepper, seeded and cut for skewering

¾	cup vegetable oil
¼	cup tamari (soy sauce)
¼	cup honey
2	T apple cider vinegar

4	hero rolls *(we prefer French)*
	butter

1	8 ounce can unsweetened pineapple chunks, drained

2	T minced onion
1	clove garlic, minced
1	t ground ginger

PREPARATION:

(a) Mix oil, tamari, honey, vinegar, onion, garlic and ginger. Add beef chunks and refrigerate for several hours.

(b) Alternate on individual skewers several pieces of beef, onions, peppers and pineapple, making each serving the length of the French roll.

(c) Place filled skewers on heated grill.

(d) Open rolls, (but do not cut through); butter inside of each roll. Lay open on grill to toast.

(e) When beef is grilled to your liking, place roll around skewer and pull off the kabobs into the toasted roll.

Speidis

Speidis are as popular in New York's Southern Tier as walk-away shrimp cocktails are on the West Coast. Part of the fun of eating this unusual sandwich comes from pulling the hot, savory marinated meat chunks off the skewer into a large slice of buttered Italian bread.

INGREDIENTS: *Serves 4 - 6*

2	pounds lean beef, cut in 1″ cubes			
2	pounds lean pork, cut in 1″ cubes			

2	cups vegetable oil	2	T crushed oregano
½	cup apple cider vinegar	1	T rosemary
1	t salt	1	t celery salt
4	t pepper	1	t basil
2	medium onions, minced	1	T dried chopped parsley
2	cloves garlic, minced	1	bay leaf, crushed

1   large loaf sliced Italian bread
     butter or margarine

PREPARATION:

(a)   After meat is cut into cubes, place in a container for marinating.

(b)   Mix all other ingredients and pour over meat. Stir so that all meat is coated with marinade. Refrigerate at least overnight *(preferably 2 or 3 days)*, tightly covered. Stir occasionally.

(c)   To barbecue, arrange on skewers and grill for 8 to 15 minutes. Serve in slices of buttered Italian bread.

Hot Cheese and Chinook

When Indian summer days keep you out of doors, you may need a quick dinner idea. Try this one!

INGREDIENTS: *Serves 4*

½	cup mayonnaise
¼	cup Parmesan cheese, grated
½	t onion powder
1	t dry mustard
1	15½ ounce can salmon, drained and flaked
4	whole wheat hamburger buns
	fresh parsley, chopped

PREPARATION:

(a) Mix ingredients and spread on buns.

(b) Place under preheated broiler for about 2 minutes or until golden brown.

(c) Sprinkle parsley over tops before serving.

HOME BAKERY

Home Bakery

Breads and Muffins

Home Bakery

Breads and Muffins

In her book "The Sense of Wonder", Rachel Carson says that, "the sense of smell, almost more than any other, has the power to recall memories . . ." We believe that helping our children to build happy memories is a big part of helping them to grow into happy, successful adults. We want our children to remember good, happy childhood times, mingled with the warm smells of wholesome foods lovingly prepared.

We find great satisfaction in providing our families with the goodness of home-baked muffins, breads, biscuits and other quick breads. Like many others who are seeking to improve their family's diet and nutrition, we choose to use the very best ingredients in their most natural form as much as possible.

The golden wheat fields of Eastern Oregon give us the ability to obtain freshly ground wheat flour. What a feeling to see the wheat growing in the seemingly endless fields, as it blows in the breezes and soaks up lots of sunshine and rain. When we make our own homemade breads and muffins it gives us the pleasure of working in partnership with nature. When whole grain flours, unprocessed bran and corn meal are combined with Oregon's abundance of filberts, walnuts, apples, berries and raw honey the results can only mean good, healthy eating.

By sharing the joy of home baking with your family you will be encouraging the next generation to choose their foods wisely and to experience a love of baking.

Chunky Applesauce Muffins

These muffins make for mighty good eating! Part of living in Oregon, to us, means using fresh local produce, as well as freezing and drying some for use throughout the year. On applesauce-making day, when the children help bring in the crisp apples and core them for the giant applesauce pot, we hope we are instilling the next generation with the satisfaction and pleasure of working in partnership with nature.

INGREDIENTS: *Makes 12 large muffins*

1¾	cups whole wheat flour
2	t baking powder
1	t cinnamon
¼	t ground ginger
1	egg, beaten
½	cup milk
⅓	cup vegetable oil
¾	cup unsweetened applesauce
2	medium apples, coarsely chopped
½	cup walnuts, coarsely chopped

PREPARATION:

(a)   Combine flour, baking powder and spices.

(b)   In another bowl mix egg, milk and oil.

(c)   Add the applesauce, apples and nuts to the dry ingredients, stirring lightly.

(d)   Add egg, milk and oil mixture and stir just until moistened. The batter should be lumpy.

(e)   Fill greased muffin pans ⅔ full. Bake at 400 degrees for 20 - 25 minutes, or until lightly browned.

Oatmeal Blueberry Muffins

Try these when bucketsful of wild mountain huckleberries may be picked free as all outdoors.

INGREDIENTS: *Makes 12 muffins*

1	cup old-fashioned oats
1	cup buttermilk or sour milk (add 1 T vinegar to a cup of milk to sour)
1/3	cup vegetable oil
1/2	cup brown sugar
1	egg
1	cup unbleached white flour
1	t baking powder
1/2	t baking soda
1/2	t salt
1	cup blueberries

PREPARATION:

(a) Mix together the oats and buttermilk and set aside.

(b) Blend together the oil, sugar and egg.

(c) In another bowl mix together the flour, baking powder, baking soda and salt. Stir this alternately with the oat mixture into the blended ingredients.

(d) Fold in the blueberries.

(e) Fill greased muffin pan ⅔ full and bake for 20 minutes at 400 degrees.

Cracked Wheat Muffins

These muffins bake into mountain peaks that show off the specks of cracked wheat. They are mighty crisp on the outside, and oh, so soft on the inside. We hope they will convey a feeling of warm satisfaction as they find their way into the hearts and tummies of your family. NOTE: Cracked wheat needs to be cooked 20 minutes ahead of muffin preparation.

INGREDIENTS: *Makes 12 muffins*

1/2	cup cracked wheat
2	cups water
2	cups unbleached white flour
3	t baking powder
1	egg
1	cup milk
4	T vegetable oil

PREPARATION:

(a) Bring water to boil and slowly add cracked wheat. Cover and reduce heat, simmer 20 minutes, stirring occasionally. Set aside while you prepare the rest of the recipe. (Store extra in a container in the refrigerator.)

(b) Measure flour and baking powder into a bowl. Add egg, milk, oil and cooked cracked wheat. Stir until free of lumps.

(c) Fill well-greased muffin pans 2/3 full and bake at 425 degrees for 25 minutes.

Maple Syrup Muffins

Baking these muffins reminds the Palmers of a trip to the country in New York to buy a supply of maple syrup. While driving through the snow-covered countryside and seeing sap buckets hanging on the sugar maple trees, the air had a feeling of anticipation of Spring soon to come. Since they're no longer living on the East coast, Eric's grandparents take this trip for them each year.

INGREDIENTS: *Makes 1 dozen*

1	cup old-fashioned oats
1	cup unbleached white flour
4	t baking powder
¼	t salt
2	eggs
½	cup milk
½	cup pure maple syrup
½	cup chopped walnuts (or pecans)

PREPARATION:

(a)   Combine dry ingredients and mix well.

(b)   Beat eggs. Add milk and syrup to eggs and blend well. Stir egg and syrup mixture into dry ingredients and blend well.

(c)   Fill greased muffin pan ⅔ full. Bake at 350 degrees for 20 minutes or until golden brown.

Apple Bran Muffins

People in the Portland area are fortunate to have the choice of either taking a leisurely drive to the Hood River apple orchards or of picking their own apples from one of the U-pick orchards close by. By serving these muffins you'll be taking a big step toward ensuring healthy bodies and sound minds for yourself and your family.

INGREDIENTS: *Makes 24 muffins*

2	cups whole wheat flour		1/2	cup raisins
1 1/2	cups unprocessed bran		1/2	cup walnuts, coarsely chopped
1 1/4	t baking soda		1/4	cup orange juice
1/2	t nutmeg		1 3/4	cups buttermilk (fresh or powdered)
1/2	t cinnamon		1	egg, beaten
2	t grated orange rind		1/2	cup unsulphured molasses
1	cup unpeeled apple, coarsely chopped		2	T vegetable oil

PREPARATION:

(a) Mix flour, bran, soda, nutmeg and cinnamon together with fork. Stir in orange rind, apples, raisins, and nuts.

(b) In another bowl mix orange juice, buttermilk, egg, molasses and oil; stir thoroughly.

(c) Mix together wet ingredients and dry ingredients with a few swift strokes.

(d) Pour into greased muffin pans, filling 2/3 full.

(e) Bake for 25 minutes at 350 degrees.

Bran Muffins with Raisins

It would be hard to think of a healthier muffin than this one. Elsie served these (along with orange juice, milk, and hard cooked eggs) to Eric and his friend, Trent, after they had slept all night in the playhouse. Trent went home and told his Mom, "That was the best breakfast I ever had!"

INGREDIENTS: *Makes 18 muffins*

2	cups unprocessed bran
¾	cup whole wheat flour
½	t baking soda
1	t grated lemon rind
2	eggs
⅓	cup unsulphured molasses
1	T vegetable oil
1¼	cups sour milk or buttermilk
¼	cup raisins

PREPARATION:

(a)   Combine dry ingredients in large bowl.

(b)   Beat eggs with molasses, oil, and milk and add to dry ingredients. Mix just until dry ingredients are moistened.

(c)   Fold in raisins.

(d)   Fill lightly greased muffin tins ⅔ full

(e)   Bake for 20 minutes at 375 degrees.

Old-Time Buttermilk Biscuits

These are four-season biscuits. They are as tempting and rewarding in June as in January — a definite must with the turkey a la king found on page 104.

INGREDIENTS: *Makes 16 medium-sized biscuits*

2	cups unbleached white flour
3	T untoasted wheat germ
3	T powdered buttermilk
1	t sugar
2½	t baking powder
½	t salt
¼	t baking soda
⅓	cup vegetable oil
¾	cup water

PREPARATION:

(a) Mix dry ingredients thoroughly. Work in the oil until mixture is of corn meal consistency.

(b) Add water and mix with fork until dough forms a ball.

(c) Roll and cut, or form dough into ½″ thick, 2″ biscuits.

(d) Bake on lightly greased baking sheet for 12 to 15 minutes at 450 degrees.

Golden Cheddar Salad Wafers

These cheesy wafers are the perfect accompaniment to a light summer meal when chef salad and fresh fruit are served. Double or triple the recipe so you can keep some in the freezer. They also make great snacks that travel well for those fun-filled summer outings.

INGREDIENTS: *Makes 5 - 6 dozen wafers*

1	pound sharp cheddar cheese
1	cup butter or margarine, softened
2½	cups unbleached white flour
½	t salt
¼	t cayenne

PREPARATION:

(a)   Blend all ingredients together with a pastry blender.

(b)   Mix well with hands and form into a roll 1 to 1½ inches in diameter. Chill for 1 to 2 hours.

(c)   Slice into ¼″ thick rounds and place on an ungreased baking sheet. Bake at 350 degrees for 10 - 12 minutes or until golden.

Mom's Johnny Cake

This corn bread recipe has been in Elsie's family for many years and brings back warm memories of childhood, when there was always something delicious just emerging from the oven. It's a good recipe for hard times as well as good times.

INGREDIENTS: *Serves 4 - 6*

2/3	cup brown sugar
2	eggs
1/2	cup vegetable shortening
2	cups unbleached white flour
1½	cups yellow corn meal
1¼	t baking soda
1	t baking powder
2	cups sour milk (To make sour milk add 2 T vinegar to milk.)

PREPARATION:

(a)   Blend brown sugar, eggs and shortening.

(b)   Mix together flour, cornmeal, baking soda and baking powder.

(c)   Add dry ingredients to the blended wet ingredients, alternating with sour milk. Mix just enough to moisten.

(d)   Pour into greased 9″ x 13″ pan.

(e)   Bake at 375 degrees for 30 minutes, or until golden brown.

Mexican Cheese and Chile Bread

This unusual bread teams well with a spicy, crunchy taco or tostada salad.

INGREDIENTS: *Serves 6*

1	cup cream style corn
¾	cup milk
⅓	cup vegetable oil
2	eggs, slightly beaten
1	cup yellow cornmeal
1	t baking powder
½	t salt
1	8 ounce can diced green chiles
1¾	cups shredded cheddar cheese

PREPARATION:

(a)   Mix corn, milk, oil and eggs.

(b)   Add cornmeal, baking powder and salt.

(c)   Pour ½ of the batter into a buttered 11¾″ x 7″ glass baking dish. Place a layer made of ½ of the chiles and ½ of the cheese on the batter.

(d)   Pour on the rest of the batter and top with remaining chiles and cheese.

(e)   Bake at 375 degrees for 45 - 50 minutes. Let cool at least 10 minutes before cutting.

Golden Nebraska Corn Bread

Jody was born and raised on a farm in Nebraska where her family grew and harvested acres of corn. After you've whipped up a batch of this corn bread you'll find it far surpasses commercially prepared package mixes.

INGREDIENTS: *Serves 4 - 6*

1	t baking soda
2	cups buttermilk (fresh or powdered)
2	cups yellow corn meal
1/4	cup vegetable oil
1	T brown sugar
2	eggs, beaten

PREPARATION:

(a) Mix the soda with a little of the buttermilk until frothy.

(b) Mix all other ingredients and add soda and buttermilk.

(c) Bake at 350 degrees in a greased 11" x 8" pan for 25 - 30 minutes, or until a toothpick inserted in center comes out clean.

(d) Cut into generous squares; serve hot with butter and honey or your favorite fruit butter.

Walnut Banana Bread

Friday after school it's nice to have a warm loaf of this banana bread waiting on the bread board when the door opens and the kids say, "What's to eat?" While looking over the week's work, with slices of warm bread and a glass of cold milk, hopefully the spices and flavorings will linger into warm memories.

INGREDIENTS: *Makes three 5½" x 3¼" loaves*

1	cup brown sugar
½	cup butter or margarine
2	T buttermilk (fresh or powdered)
1	t baking soda
2	egg yolks, beaten
1½	cups mashed bananas
½	cup walnuts, coarsely chopped
1	t cinnamon
1¾	cups whole wheat flour
2	egg whites, stiffly beaten

PREPARATION:

(a)   Cream the sugar and butter until smooth.

(b)   Dissolve the soda in the buttermilk.

(c)   Mix in egg yolks, buttermilk/soda, bananas, nuts, cinnamon and flour.

(d)   Fold in stiffly beaten egg whites.

(e)   Fill well-greased pans with batter and bake at 350 degrees for 35 - 45 minutes.

Pumpkin Gingerbread

Part of every Fall means heading to the pumpkin patch to choose the perfect pumpkins. Our rule is — if you can carry it, you can have it. How delightful it is to eat something warm made with spicy pumpkin after carving jack-o-lanterns. Pop this gingerbread into the oven before you start to carve, and enjoy a happy ending.

INGREDIENTS: *Serves 4 - 6*

½	cup vegetable oil
½	cup brown sugar
1	egg
½	cup unsulphured molasses
1	cup buttermilk (fresh or powdered)
½	cup canned pumpkin
2¼	cups unbleached white flour
1	t baking soda
1½	t ginger
1½	t cinnamon

PREPARATION:

(a)   Blend together the oil and brown sugar.

(b)   Continue to beat and add: the egg, molasses, buttermilk and pumpkin. Beat all the air you can into the batter at this time.

(c)   Stir the dry ingredients into the batter and beat just until smooth. Do not over-beat. Pour into greased 9″ square pan.

(d)   Bake at 350 degrees for 40 - 45 minutes.

Gingerbread

This is the kind of recipe that really grows on you. It's dark and rich with molasses and fragrant spices. Prepare it for your family carefully and lovingly and they'll be sure to come back for more!

INGREDIENTS: *Serves 6 - 8*

¾	cup honey
¾	cup vegetable oil
1	cup unsulphured molasses
3	eggs
3	cups whole wheat flour
1	t ground cloves
3	t baking powder
1	t ground ginger
1½	t cinnamon
2	cups milk

PREPARATION:

(a)   Mix honey, oil, molasses and eggs. Set aside.

(b)   Sift together all dry ingredients.

(c)   Add flour mixture to honey mixture alternately with milk.

(d)   Pour into greased 9″ x 13″ pan. Bake at 350 degrees for 45 - 50 minutes.

Chunky Apple Bread

A little boy would do just about anything to get another hunk of this freshly baked apple bread. Jody's son, Eric, often sneaks back into the kitchen when it's "too close to dinner" for "just one more piece, please?" It's no wonder he can't resist, because the cinnamon fragrance is so tantalizing.

INGREDIENTS: *Makes one 9½" x 5½" loaf*

½	cup butter or margarine
1	cup brown sugar
2	eggs, beaten
1¾	cups plus 2T unbleached white flour
2	T untoasted wheat germ
2	cups apples, coarsely chopped
½	cup walnuts, coarsely chopped
1	t vanilla
1	t baking soda
1½	t milk
2	t cinnamon

PREPARATION:

(a) Cream butter and sugar. Add eggs, flour, wheat germ, apples, nuts and vanilla.

(b) Mix soda and milk together and add along with cinnamon.

(c) Put in well-greased bread pan and sprinkle the top heavily with additional cinnamon. Batter will be thick.

(d) Bake at 350 degrees for 40 - 45 minutes.

Onion Biscuit Bread

This is one of those nothing-can-go-wrong recipes. If you have been a slave to packaged mixes or brown and serve rolls this will show you that "make-from-scratch" is quick, easy and more economical. This bread is great with hot soup on a chilly evening.

INGREDIENTS: *Serves 4 - 6*

2	cups unbleached white flour
2	T untoasted wheat germ
3	t baking powder
¼	t salt
½	cup dried minced onions
4	T vegetable oil
⅔-¾	cup milk
3	T butter or margarine, softened
3	T sesame seeds

PREPARATION:

(a)   Blend together flour, wheat germ, baking powder, salt and minced onions.

(b)   With a table knife blend in oil, then milk, until well blended.

(c)   Place a small amount of additional flour on clean surface (wherever you generally roll out biscuit or pie dough). Knead dough slightly until smooth on the outside.

(d)   Place dough on an ungreased cookie sheet and with a rolling pin roll into an oblong ½ inch thick. Dough will not completely fill the pan.

(e)   Spread softened butter over the dough and sprinkle with sesame seeds. Bake at 425 degrees for 15 - 17 minutes, or until golden brown. Cut into squares for serving.

No-Knead Coffee Can Bread

This batter bread is fun to make. Children enjoy watching to see when the lids will push off, indicating it's time to bake the bread. This bread is best fresh from the oven, but the round slices also make terrific toast.

INGREDIENTS: *Makes 2 small coffee-can-size loaves*

1	package active dry yeast		1	t salt
½	cup warm water		1	egg, slightly beaten
1	cup milk, scalded		1	cup Instant Roman Meal cereal
2	T butter or margarine		2	cups unbleached white flour
2	T unsulphured molasses		1	cup whole wheat flour

PREPARATION:

(a) In large bowl of electric mixer, dissolve the yeast in water. Add butter to scalded milk; set aside and cool to lukewarm.

(b) Stir in molasses, salt and egg. Add milk mixture to yeast, then blend in cereal.

(c) With mixer on low speed, gradually beat in 1 cup of white and the 1 cup of whole wheat flour; beat 2 minutes.

(d) Mix in the remaining one cup flour with heavy wooden spoon until dough is very elastic.

(e) Place dough in two one-pound coffee cans that are very well greased. Also grease the lids and put them on. Let rise in warm place until lids pop off.

(f) Set lids aside. Bake at 350 degrees 40 - 45 minutes, until crust is well browned. Cool in the cans 10 minutes, then remove. Cool upright.

Cookie Dough Style Granola

We are including a granola recipe in this section of the book because it's the best we've ever tasted. If you love to snitch cookie dough, your taste buds should not go on without tasting this moist, high-fiber granola. This is a regular in our homes. It replaces the over-processed, enriched, chemical-laden cereals so readily available at the supermarket.

INGREDIENTS: *Makes 7 quarts*

2⅓	cups brown sugar (or 1 cup honey and ¾ cup pure maple syrup)	1	large carton old-fashioned oats	
		1	cup untoasted wheat germ	
1½	cups cold water (omit if you use honey and maple syrup)	1	pound flaked coconut	
		2	cups unsalted sunflower seeds	
1½	cups vegetable oil	2	cups chopped nuts (walnuts, pecans or almonds)	
2	T vanilla			
3	T cinnamon	2	cups raisins (optional)	

PREPARATION:

(a)   Heat in large Dutch oven the brown sugar (or honey/maple syrup), water, oil, vanilla and cinnamon. Stir until dissolved then remove from heat.

(b)   Add all other ingredients except raisins and blend well.

(c)   Divide granola between two baking sheets and bake each at 350 degrees for 10 minutes.

(d)   After baking add raisins if you desire.

(e)   Cool and store in container or jar in the refrigerator or freezer. This will keep for six weeks in the refrigerator.

FAVORITE ENTREES

Cook's Choice

Favorite Entrées

Cook's Choice

Favorite Entrees

We include in this section of the book favorites from our kitchens. Here are some suggestions for days when you wonder, "What can I serve that is different?" We also include some "serve with" suggestions which may help to free your mind of some of the menu planning. We hope that using some of these "choices" will mean more time for you and less last-minute stress after a day of busy activities.

With the fast pace of today's crowded schedules families sometimes need meals that are fast to fix, easy and well-balanced. Here are some dishes that make family meal preparation easy. You will notice the absence of many commercially prepared ingredients that contain large amounts of salt, sugar and some unnecessary chemical additives and preservatives. If you feed your family with high regard for good nutrition, their good mental and physical health will be your reward many times over.

We believe that part of "eating the Oregon way" includes presenting meals with the style and ease they deserve. Whether we are eating at the beach, the mountains or beside a misty waterfall we like to add little extra touches that make eating more enjoyable. Serving meals on the patio, in front of a cozy fire or from a picnic basket will enhance your mealtime pleasure and is bound to be appreciated and long-remembered.

Crab Broccoli Pie

When Jody first moved to Oregon several years ago she was anxious to experience as many things as possible that make Oregon such an ideal place to be. One rainy day their family went to Waldport, Oregon, which is a terrific place for crabbing. What fun it was to pull up the crab pots and hurry to grab the big ones before they scurried back into the bay!

Sometime when you have out-of-town guests, serve this crab pie for a luncheon. It will give them a taste of Oregon, and you don't even have to catch your own crab; you can use frozen or canned.

INGREDIENTS: *Makes on 9" pie*

Crust:

1¼	cups unbleached white flour		½	cup butter or margarine
2	t baking powder		¼	cup milk
½	t salt		1	T chives, chopped

Crab Filling:

1	cup crab meat		1	cup cheddar cheese, shredded
3	hard-cooked eggs, diced		1	cup mayonnaise
½	cup celery, chopped		1	10 ounce package diced broccoli, slightly cooked and drained
2	T green onions, sliced			

PREPARATION:

(a) Prepare crust by mixing flour, baking powder and salt; cut in butter. Add milk and chives, stirring until a ball forms. Pat into 9" pie pan.

(b) Fold together crab meat, eggs, celery, onion, cheese and mayonnaise.

(c) Place broccoli in bottom of pastry-lined pan. Spoon crab mixture over the top.

(d) Bake at 375 degrees for 30 minutes, or until golden brown.

Baked Stuffed Salmon

Tradition has it that for centuries Northwest Indians have been catching salmon and baking it over open fire pits on redwood stakes. With today's modern conveniences it's easy for us to enjoy salmon any time.

INGREDIENTS: *Serves 6 - 8*

1	3 - 5 pound dressed salmon
	salt to taste
	freshly ground pepper
1	large onion, sliced
1	lemon, thinly sliced
1	bunch fresh parsley, cleaned
3	slices bacon

PREPARATION:

(a) Line a baking dish with a piece of foil which is large enough to cover openings of salmon after prepared. Grease the foil, then place the salmon on the foil. Sprinkle cavity with desired amount of salt and pepper.

(b) In the cavity of the salmon layer onion, lemon slices and parsley. Press foil which is lining the dish around the opening of the cavity to hold it together, but do not cover the top.

(c) Arrange the bacon slices over the top of the salmon.

(d) Bake uncovered at 350 degrees for 45 to 60 minutes, or until fish flakes when tested with a fork. Skin is easily removed before serving if desired.

Sue's Sole

A stop at the local fish market where one can see live crab, lobster and steamer clams is something our children look forward to. Often our seafood choice is the delicate fresh Pacific sole. We hope this crispy, cheese-baked dish will become one of your favorites.

INGREDIENTS: *Serves 4 - 6*

½ cup butter or margarine	⅓ cup Italian seasoned bread crumbs
1-1½ pounds sole, cut into bite-size pieces	¼ cup Parmesan cheese, grated
2 eggs, beaten	1-1½ cups Swiss cheese, grated
1 T milk	fresh parsley

PREPARATION:

(a) Heat oven to 400 degrees. Put the butter in the bottom of a large baking dish and melt it in the oven that is pre-heating.

(b) In one bowl beat the eggs and milk; set aside.

(c) In another bowl mix bread crumbs and Parmesan cheese and set aside.

(d) Take fish pieces and dip first into egg mixture, then into crumbs and Parmesan cheese. Put fish pieces in baking dish in the butter; then flip over the pieces so butter is on both sides of each fish piece.

(e) Place grated Swiss cheese evenly over prepared fish and bake on medium-high oven shelf for 15 minutes or until golden brown.

(f) Sprinkle fresh parsley over the top before serving.

Scallops Fettuccini

Jody's husband, Ed, worked with this recipe over and over until he had just the right flavor combinations. He usually cooks by taste instead of measurement, so we had to prevail upon him to get the exact measurements for this recipe.

INGREDIENTS: *Serves 6 - 8*

1	pound fettuccini noodles		3	cloves garlic, minced
1/3	cup dry white wine		3	T unbleached white flour
2	T green onion, chopped		1/2	t salt
1/2	pound scallops, cut into small pieces		1 1/2	cups half and half
1	cup fresh mushrooms, sliced		1/2	cup Swiss cheese, grated
3	T butter or margarine		3	T fresh parsley, chopped

PREPARATION:

(a) Cook fettuccini according to package directions.

(b) In saucepan, combine wine, onion, scallops and mushrooms. Cover and simmer 5 minutes; drain off most of the liquid.

(c) While that is simmering melt butter in skillet and saute garlic. Stir in flour and salt. Add half and half; cook, stirring constantly until thickened. Add Swiss cheese, then add scallop/mushroom mixture.

(d) Gently toss scallop mixture with cooked and drained fettuccini noodles.

(e) Garnish with fresh parsley.

Quick Snow Crab Bake

Elsie's mother-in-law, Mary Cambern, first served this delicious dish on New Year's Day at their home overlooking Lake Washington in Seattle. It instantly became a favorite with family and friends.

INGREDIENTS: *Serves 6*

8	ounces Snow crab
4½	ounces shrimp
4	hard-cooked eggs, sliced
½	cup celery, chopped
2	T green onion, sliced
1	cup soft, coarse whole wheat bread crumbs
1	cup sour cream
¾	cup mayonnaise
	freshly ground pepper
½	cup fine whole wheat bread crumbs (use blender to make very fine crumbs)
	parsley for garnish

PREPARATION:

(a) Break up crab meat. (If canned crab is being used, drain well.) Combine crab and shrimp with all other ingredients except ½ cup of crumbs and parsley.

(b) Place mixture in shallow buttered baking dish. Sprinkle fine bread crumbs over top.

(c) Bake at 350 degrees for 25 - 30 minutes. Garnish with parsley before serving.

NOTE: All ingredients can be placed in a large bowl ahead of time, then mixed just before baking. Have your children slice fresh fruit and arrange on your favorite fruit tray; then serve with a basketful of warm bran-raisin muffins for a beautiful, yet simple meal.

Salmon Quiche

"Fish on! Fish on! Get the net!" That's the cry of one who has just hooked an ocean salmon. As the salmon is reeled in amidst cheers and applause, one no longer minds having had to be at the boat dock at such an early pre-dawn hour. After the fresh salmon has been eaten and enjoyed, use what is left over for this "special day" quiche.

INGREDIENTS: *Makes one 9" quiche*

1	pie crust, baked 3 - 5 minutes at 400 degrees
½	pound cooked salmon or 18 ounce can salmon, drained and flaked
1	cup Swiss cheese, grated
¼	cup Parmesan cheese, grated
4	green onions, sliced
3	eggs
1	cup milk
	dash cayenne

PREPARATION:

(a) In the partially baked pie crust layer first salmon, then Swiss cheese, Parmesan cheese and green onions.

(b) Beat together eggs, milk and cayenne. Pour over other ingredients in crust.

(c) Bake for 45 minutes at 350 degrees. Allow to cool for 10 minutes before serving.

Chicken Pot Pie
With Make in the Pan, No-Roll Crust

Watch the way everyone hustles around to help set up for dinner when this hot, irresistible chicken pot pie is baking in the oven. Do you remember sitting as a child wide-eyed and eager while your mother brought a steaming-hot meat pie to the table? No one can forget such home scenes and scents. Enjoy!

INGREDIENTS: *Serves 4 - 6*

Crust:

1½	cups unbleached white flour			
1	t sugar	2	T milk	
½	t salt	½	cup vegetable oil	

Mix in 10″ pie pan and pat to fit pan. Make one more crust (this time mix in a bowl) to be crumbled over the top of the pot pie.

1½	cups homemade chicken stock, fat-skimmed	1	cup carrots, diced and cooked until almost tender, and drained
1½	cups milk		salt to taste
½	cup unbleached white flour		freshly ground pepper
3	cups cooked chicken or turkey, diced		
1	large onion, chopped		
1	10 ounce package frozen peas, cooked until almost tender, and drained		

PREPARATION:

(a)   Bring to a boil over moderate heat the chicken stock and 1 cup of the milk. Blend together the remaining ½ cup of milk and the flour; quickly stir into boiling mixture. Boil 1 minute, stirring constantly. Remove from heat; stir in salt and pepper and fold in all other ingredients.

(b)   Pour filling into pastry-lined pie pan and top with crumbled top crust.

(c)   Bake in 400 degree oven for 45 - 55 minutes or until golden brown.

Garlic Skillet Chicken

The first time Elsie cooked this chicken it was a warm summer day and the kitchen window was open, letting the savory aroma drift out to the street. Her neighbor, Kellie, was just walking by, taking her little girls for a walk. She came to the window sniffing and asked, "What are you cooking? It smells so good!" This may sound like a lot of garlic. However, the cooking, along with the soy sauce, mellows the flavor into a dark, glazed finish.

INGREDIENTS: *Serves 4 - 6*

4	pounds chicken pieces
4	T vegetable oil
20	garlic cloves, peeled
4	whole dried hot red peppers
3	T honey
¼	cup tamari (soy sauce)
¾	cup white wine vinegar

PREPARATION:

(a) After the chicken is washed, cut pieces to uniform size with a heavy serrated knife or cleaver. In a heavy skillet brown the pieces well in the vegetable oil.

(b) Add the garlic and whole hot peppers and cook a little longer, until lightly browned. Add remaining ingredients and cook over medium heat until chicken is done and glazed with the sauce. Turn chicken pieces several times during cooking.

(c) Remove hot peppers and serve.

Turkey A La King
With Buttermilk Biscuits

If the people who eat at your table are biscuit lovers, count on their asking for this creamy turkey and biscuit dinner again and again.

INGREDIENTS: *Serves 4*

¼	cup butter or margarine
1	8 ounce can mushroom stems and pieces, drained
⅓	cup green pepper, chopped
¼	cup unbleached white flour
½	t salt
	freshly ground pepper
1	cup homemade chicken stock, fat-skimmed
1	cup half and half
1	cup cooked turkey (or chicken), diced

PREPARATION:

(a)   In butter sauté mushrooms and green pepper. Blend in flour and seasonings. Cook over low heat, stirring until mixture is smooth and bubbly. Remove from the heat.

(b)   Slowly add the stock and half and half. Bring to a boil over low heat, stirring constantly. Boil one minute.

(c)   Add the turkey (or chicken). Continue cooking until the meat is thoroughly heated.

(d)   Serve with buttermilk biscuits (or rice or noodles).

NOTE: The recipe for Buttermilk Biscuits is found on page 80.

Ann's Chicken Rolls

If you're ever in a quandary about what to serve a crowd, here's a suggestion. Ann Tripple, who gave us this recipe, has served this chicken to as many as 50 people. Preparing them a day ahead improves flavor and texture; then bake just before serving.

INGREDIENTS:

6	chicken breast halves, boned and skinned*
1	pint sour cream
1	8 ounce box Ritz cheese crackers
	fresh parsley for garnish

NOTE: When chicken breasts are boned you will have 1 large piece of meat and 1 smaller piece. When rolling the chicken use two of the smaller pieces together to make a roll. The larger pieces will each make one roll.

PREPARATION:

(a)   Crush the crackers to make very fine crumbs (or blend in the blender). Spread crumbs on a plate.

(b)   Spread sour cream on one side of each chicken breast, then dip in crumbs to coat. Spread other side with sour cream, dip in crumbs, then roll up.

(c)   Place rolls seam side down in lightly greased baking dish and bake for 1 hour at 300 degrees.

(d)   Transfer chicken rolls to serving dish and garnish with parsley.

Ten Minute Chicken Stir Fry

When you are especially hungry for vegetables, this is the meal to fix. Using pre-cooked chicken makes it a breeze to prepare. Our children readily eat their vegetables on nights when this is served.

INGREDIENTS: *Serves 6*

3	T vegetable oil		1	medium onion, chopped
1½	cups cooked chicken, cut into bite-size pieces		1	8 ounce can mushroom stems and pieces, drained; reserve liquid
3	T tamari (soy sauce)		2	cloves garlic, minced
1	cup carrots, sliced diagonally		½	cup cold water
1	cup celery, sliced diagonally		2	T cornstarch
1	10 ounce package frozen pea pods			salt to taste
1	green pepper, cut into bite-size pieces			freshly ground pepper

PREPARATION:

(a)   Heat 1 T oil in wok or fry pan at 375 degrees.

(b)   Add carrots and celery and stir-fry about 2 minutes. Add reserved mushroom liquid, cover and steam about 4 minutes. Remove carrots.

(c)   Heat 1 T oil in wok. Add pea pods, stir-fry about 2 minutes and push up to one side. Add onions, mushrooms, and garlic. Stir-fry 2 minutes. Push to another side. Heat 1 T oil in wok. Add chicken and soy sauce; stir-fry 2 minutes. Add carrots.

(d)   Combine water and cornstarch. Stir into meat mixture and cook until thickened. Reduce heat to warm for serving.

NOTE: This tastes great when served with long or short grain brown rice and a salad.

Chicken Piccata

In keeping with the recommendation of the American Heart Association to control the amount and type of fat you eat by using fish, chicken, turkey, and veal in most of your meat meals for the week, here's another that you may wish to add to your list of favorites.

INGREDIENTS: *Serves 4 - 6*

4	whole chicken breasts, halved, skinned and boned		2	T olive oil
½	cup unbleached white flour		3	T water
	salt to taste		3	T lemon juice
	freshly ground pepper		4	T capers
¼	cup butter or margarine			fresh parsley, chopped for garnish

PREPARATION:

(a) Place several pieces of the chicken at a time between two sheets of waxed paper, leaving room for the meat to expand. Pound each piece gently but firmly with a flat-surfaced mallet until about $\frac{3}{16}$-inch thick.

(b) Combine flour, salt and pepper in a bag; add flattened chicken breasts and shake to coat lightly.

(c) Place a 10 to 12-inch skillet over high heat. When hot, coat surface with part of the butter and olive oil. Saute' chicken breasts, a few at a time, 2 or 3 minutes on each side, adding more butter and olive oil as pan appears dry. Drain meat on paper towels and keep warm.

(d) When meat is all cooked, drain off all but 2 T of butter and oil. Stir in water and lemon juice and scrape bottom to loosen browned bits. Return meat to skillet and heat until sauce thickens. Add capers; then remove to platter for serving. Garnish with chopped parsley.

Chicken-Pineapple Teriyaki

As the chicken pieces marinate and cook they soak up the teriyaki sauce. Enjoy the taste combinations as you savor each bite-size tasty morsel of the chicken and pineapple. It's fun to cook these on a hibachi and let each guest brown them to his own liking.

INGREDIENTS: *Serves 4*

Marinade:
½   cup tamari (soy sauce)
¼   cup cooking sherry (or white grape juice)
2   T brown sugar
¼   t dry mustard
1   clove garlic, minced
½   t ground ginger

3   whole chicken breasts, boned, skinned and cubed
2   cups fresh pineapple, cubed

PREPARATION:

(a)   Mix all marinade ingredients in a medium-sized bowl.

(b)   Place prepared chicken pieces into marinade and let set for at least an hour.

(c)   Just before cooking alternate pieces of chicken and pineapple on wooden skewers.

(d)   Cook over hibachi, or broil 4 inches from heat for 3 - 5 minutes. During cooking time baste once or twice with marinade.

Western Beef Brisket

The all-time favorite summer barbeque flavor penetrates every ounce of these tender beef slices. It's a real favorite of many Westerners.

INGREDIENTS: *Serves 4 - 6*

4	pounds beef brisket, trimmed of all fat
1	t hickory flavored liquid smoke
½	cup vermouth (or 3 T white wine vinegar and water to make ½ cup)
1	large onion, sliced
1	t garlic powder as desired
1	cooking bag
	hickory flavored barbeque sauce

PREPARATION:

(a) Place meat in cooking bag. Cover with onions and pour in liquid smoke and vermouth. Sprinkle with garlic powder.

(b) Place bag in the refrigerator to marinate for at least 6 hours.

(c) Cook at 250 degrees for 4 - 5 hours. Be sure to follow instructions on package for using cooking bag.

(d) After the meat has cooked and is very tender, carefully transfer meat from the bag to a baking pan.

(e) Pour over the meat a generous amount of barbeque sauce and put back into the oven for about 45 minutes at 300 degrees.

(f) Let the meat set out of the oven for about 10 minutes, then slice very thin.

(g) Heat extra barbeque sauce to serve with the meat.

Beef Stroganoff

Introduce this to your family; they'll ask for a repeat. It's especially good in chilly weather.

INGREDIENTS: *Serves 4 - 6*

¼	cup butter or margarine
1	large onion, chopped
1	8 ounce can sliced mushrooms, drained
1½	pounds round steak (about ½" thick), tenderized, cut into cubes
¼	cup unbleached white flour
¼	t salt
2	cups homemade beef stock, fat-skimmed
1	cup sour cream

PREPARATION:

(a)   Sauté onion in butter until transparent. Add mushrooms and continue cooking until warmed through.

(b)   Toss meat in the flour to coat, then add to sautéed vegetables and cook until well browned.

(c)   Add salt and beef stock; then simmer for about 45 minutes, stirring occasionally. Add sour cream and cook only until heated.

(d)   Serve over noodles or rice.

Teriyaki Ramaki

Children seem to love something out of the ordinary. When these tasty bites of meat and water chestnuts are broiled on skewers, the fanfare and change turn dinner into a special affair. In order to allow the flavors to blend and mellow, marinate the meat a few hours in advance.

INGREDIENTS: *Serves 4 - 6*

1½	pounds round steak, ½″ thick
¾	cup vegetable oil
¼	cup tamari (soy sauce)
¼	cup honey
2	T apple cider vinegar
2	T minced onion
1	clove garlic, minced
1	t ground ginger
1	8 ounce can whole water chestnuts

PREPARATION:

(a)   Slice round steak across the grain in very thin slices.

(b)   Combine and mix well all over ingredients except water chestnuts. Pour over meat, mix and refrigerate for several hours.

(c)   Wrap each water chestnut in a slice of the steak and fasten with a wooden skewer or pick.

(d)   Broil for 2 or 3 minutes four inches from heat.

Marinated Pork Roast

You'll enjoy the tantalizing aroma as this meat cooks in the oven. The old-fashioned eating quality reminds us of pork fresh from the farm that our mothers used to cook.

INGREDIENTS: *Serves 4 - 6*

½	cup tamari (soy sauce)
½	cup cooking sherry (1 T white wine vinegar and white grape juice to make ½ cup)
2	cloves garlic, minced
1	T dry mustard
1	t ground ginger
1	t thyme
1	4 - 5 pound boned, rolled and tied pork loin roast

PREPARATION:

(a) Combine soy sauce, sherry, garlic, mustard, ginger and thyme. Place roast in a large clear plastic bag; set in deep bowl to steady roast. Pour in marinade and close bag tightly. Let stand 2 - 3 hours at room temperature or overnight in refrigerator. Occasionally press bag against meat to distribute the marinade evenly.

(b) Remove meat from marinade. Place roast on rack in shallow roasting pan. Roast at 325 degrees for 2½ - 3 hours or until meat thermometer registers 175 degrees. Baste occasionally with marinade during last part of roasting time.

Sweet and Sour Pork

Try this — just take our word for it — and you'll cook it often in cold days to come.

INGREDIENTS: *Serves 4 - 6*

3	cups cooked pork, cut into bite-size pieces
3	T vegetable oil
1	large onion, sliced
¼	cup brown sugar
⅓	cup apple cider vinegar

2	T tamari (soy sauce)
1	20 ounce can unsweetened pineapple chunks
1	green pepper, cut into strips
2	T cornstarch

PREPARATION:

(a) In a large skillet saute the sliced onion in the oil, until transparent.

(b) Add the brown sugar, vinegar, soy sauce, green pepper, pork, pineapple and half of the juice from the can.

(c) Simmer for 20 minutes, adding a small amount of water if needed.

(d) Mix the remaining pineapple juice and cornstarch; stir into the simmering ingredients above. Continue cooking only until thickened.

(e) Serve over hot cooked rice.

NOTE: If you do not have cooked pork (such as leftover meat from a pork roast), cook any lean pork by cutting into strips, then sauteing in oil. Cover and cook for 10 to 15 minutes until tender and well-done.

Vegetable-Sausage Stir Fry

On a frosty, cold evening try this hearty dinner idea. Remember, you could eat all of the vegetables raw, so just cook them slightly.

INGREDIENTS: *Serves 6*

2	T vegetable oil
3	German sausages, broiled or grilled and cut into bite-size pieces
1	large onion, thickly sliced and quartered
1	large green pepper, cut into 1-inch pieces
1	cup celery, sliced diagonally
2	medium tomatoes, quartered
1	cup homemade beef stock, fat-skimmed
1	8 ounce can unsweetened pineapple chunks
1/4	t garlic powder
	freshly ground pepper
1	T brown sugar
2	T cornstarch
4	cups hot cooked brown rice

PREPARATION:

(a) In a large skillet heat the oil, then sauté the sausage pieces, onion, green pepper and celery. Cook just until the vegetables are tender crisp.

(b) In the meantime drain the pineapple and reserve the juice.

(c) To the sausage and vegetables add the tomatoes, broth, pineapple and seasonings. Cover and simmer 3 - 5 minutes.

(d) Blend the brown sugar and cornstarch with the reserved pineapple juice. Pour into meat-vegetable mixture and cook until thickened and clear.

(e) Serve over the hot cooked rice.

Ed's German Sausage

The combination of Ed's German origin and Jody's memories of homemade sausages hanging in the smokehouse back in Nebraska made this a natural family favorite. The process is easy and the results delicious. You also have the advantage of knowing what goes into your sausage.

INGREDIENTS: _Freeze in family-size packages_

Natural hog casing (available from butcher supply companies)

5	pounds freshly ground beef			
10	pounds freshly ground pork shoulder	3	cloves garlic, minced
3	T salt	½	cup fresh parsley, chopped
2	t pepper	1	cup Parmesan cheese, grated
2	t dry mustard	3	T Italian herb seasoning
1	cup dry white wine	2	T hickory flavored liquid smoke

PREPARATION:

(a) The sausage casings come thoroughly cleaned and packed in salt. Rinse well in cool water to remove the salt. Then soak them in clear water while preparing meat.

(b) In a very large container mix the meat with all other ingredients. (We use our hands.)

(c) When thoroughly mixed, make a small meat pattie and fry it for a taste test.

(d) Adjust seasonings until you have the perfect combination. At this point you can either shape the meat into patties or proceed with directions for stuffing.

(e) To stuff the casing, tie one end securely. Then fit open end over nozzle of stuffer and pull casing over the nozzle until you have reached the tied end. Push meat through stuffer, twist casings at the end of each desired length (about 5 - 6 inches). Be sure to stuff casing tight and free from air.

(f) Optional: For hickory smoked flavor we put uncooked sausages in a smoker for 45 minutes. The hickory smoke gives that extra zest we so love. If you have extra casings freeze them for future use.

Make-in-the-Oven Beef Sausage

Anytime you make something yourself, it's bound to be better, and you know what's in it! Having your children help make this sausage brings opportunities for them to learn the value of choosing and using your own ingredients versus settling for fillers, questionable grades of meat, artificial coloring and other additives in processed meats. When done, this sausage will have the characteristic red color of commercially made sausage.

INGREDIENTS: *Makes 5 sausage rolls*

5	pounds ground beef
5	t meat curing salt
2½	t garlic powder
2½	t coarse pepper (To break peppercorns into coarse pieces, place in a small plastic bag and pound with a meat mallet.)

1½	t mustard seeds
1	t hickory smoked salt

PREPARATION:

(a) Add all seasonings to the beef and mix well. Refrigerate for one day.

(b) Second day — mix well and return to refrigerator.

(c) Third day — mix well and shape into five rolls about 2½″ in diameter.

(d) Place on a broiler pan (so that meat doesn't sit in the drippings). Bake for 8 hours at 150 degrees, turning every two hours.

(e) Cool on paper towels placed on cooling rack, then chill or wrap individually and freeze.

NOTE: For a satisfying meal serve slices of this sausage with a green salad, soup or in a sandwich.

Thanks to Mary Ann Lawrence for sharing this recipe.

New York Style Spaghetti Sauce

In the Southern Tier area of New York State Italian restaurants reflect an Old World style of cooking which is unique to that place alone. The aroma of this spaghetti sauce cooking is sure to conjur up memories of such places which you have visited and experienced.

INGREDIENTS: *Serves 8 - 10*

3	T olive oil
1	large onion, chopped
½	green pepper, chopped
2	cloves garlic
1	4 ounce can sliced mushrooms, drained
1	pound lean ground beef
1	29 ounce can tomato sauce
1	12 ounce can tomato paste
1½	cups water
1	t chili powder
1	t ground oregano

PREPARATION:

(a)   Heat olive oil; add onion, pepper and garlic and sauté until tender.

(b)   Add mushrooms and ground beef and cook until meat is browned and crumbled.

(c)   Add remaining ingredients and stir well. Simmer for 3 - 5 hours, stirring occasionally.

FAMILY DESSERTS

Happy Endings

Family Desserts

Happy Endings

Family Desserts/Company Desserts

In this chapter you will find suggestions for happy mealtime endings. When a dessert is served, it should be planned as an integral part of the meal, keeping in mind that your body is only as good as what you put into it. When a wholesome meal is prepared and served, your family will feel loved, warm and happily filled.

In the section on Family Desserts there are recipes that we choose to serve our families. We heartily agree with the current trend to cut down on the use of sugars and sweets. Therefore, in order to establish good eating habits we plan our family desserts around the use of fresh Oregon fruits, berries, nuts and farm fresh dairy products.

Occasionally there are times when we enjoy serving sweet and tempting desserts to our guests. In the Company Desserts section are recipes that feature that all-time favorite flavor — chocolate, plus warm fruit desserts, pies, cakes and other special treats laced with liqueurs.

We know that in the busy pace of today's world it's sometimes necessary and more convenient to take advantage of prepared desserts. But, no matter where you may search for that beautiful, extra-delicious dessert, you'll have a hard time surpassing the pride and pleasure of serving one made from scratch in your very own kitchen.

Mid-Summer Blueberry Pie

Blueberry picking days are so special — as much fun as any summer outing. The blueberry bushes at our favorite blueberry farms are usually weighed down with huge, perfect berries. It's hard to stop picking when it's time to quit and take the loaded carriers to be weighed. Somehow those remaining berries just "beg" to be picked.

INGREDIENTS: *Makes one 8" pie*

1	8" pie shell, baked and cooled		
1½	quarts fresh or frozen blueberries	3	T cornstarch
1	cup sugar	1	t cinnamon

PREPARATION:

(a)   In bottom of pie shell place half of the uncooked berries.

(b)   Place remaining berries in a saucepan. Pour sugar over berries, and mix lightly. Place pan over low heat and slowly bring to a boil.

(c)   Mix the cornstarch with just enough water to dissolve, then add to the berries. Continue cooking, stirring continually, until thickened and clear — about 3 minutes. Stir in cinnamon.

(d)   Cool for about 10 or 15 minutes; then pour over fresh berries in shell. Chill. Serve topped with whipped cream or ice cream, if desired.

NOTE: *To freeze fresh-picked blueberries, immediately sort out any over-ripe or soft berries (to be used right away). Place berries to be frozen into storage bags (using 11½" x 13" size), unwashed and dry. The berries will stay loose so that you can easily remove any amount desired, rinse and use in your favorite recipes.*

Oregon Peach Pie

A warm summer evening, a peach pie and good friends are three joys to sample together.

INGREDIENTS: *Makes one 9″ pie*

No-Roll Bottom Crust:

1½	cups unbleached white flour	2	T milk
1	t sugar	½	cup vegetable oil
½	t salt		

Filling:

½	cup sugar	1	t cinnamon
¼	cup unbleached white flour	4½	cups peaches, peeled and sliced

Top Crumb Crust:

½	cup butter or margarine, softened	1	cup unbleached white flour
½	cup brown sugar		

PREPARATION:

(a) Prepare crust by mixing all crust ingredients directly in the 9″ pie pan. Pat dough to fit pan.

(b) Heat oven to 425 degrees.

(c) Mix sugar, flour and cinnamon. Mix lightly through peaches. Pour into pie pan.

(d) Mix all ingredients for top crumb crust until crumbly. Crumble over pie.

(e) Cover edge of crust with narrow strips of foil to prevent excessive browning.

(f) Bake 35 - 40 minutes or until crust is nicely browned. Serve slightly warm topped with vanilla ice cream.

Grandma Jackson's Deep-Dish Blackberry Pie

This is a homey deep-dish pie that makes the search for blackberries along fence rows pay off. We thank Ann Tripple for sharing one of her grandmother's favorite recipes with us.

INGREDIENTS: *Serves 6 - 8*

2	quarts blackberries, fresh or frozen*		3	T butter or margarine
1½	cups sugar			

Crust:

½	t salt		4	T vegetable shortening
2	cups unbleached white flour		½	cup milk

PREPARATION:

(a) Place half of the berries in a 7½″ x 12″ pan. Sprinkle half of the sugar over the berries and dot with half the butter.

(b) Prepare the crust and divide in half. Roll half of the crust into an oblong to fit the pan. Prick thoroughly to let steam escape, and place over the berries, sugar and butter.

(c) Bake at 400 degrees for 30 minutes, or until crust is golden brown.

(d) Repeat the above steps with the remaining half of the ingredients, baking another 30 minutes. The first crust will soak up the juice of the berries, making a delectable blend of berries and crust.

(e) Serve warm, topped with vanilla ice cream.

*NOTE: If frozen berries are used increase to 2½ quarts.

Old Fashioned Apple Pie

One of Elsie's favorite Fall activities when growing up in upstate New York was going to the cider mill and seeing the big cider presses producing gallons of tangy cider. Upon returning home she would be enticed into the kitchen by the mouth-watering aroma of cinnamon-rich apple pies fresh from the oven.

INGREDIENTS: *Makes on 9" pie*

Pastry for two-crust 9" pie

1	cup sugar
1	t cinnamon
½	t nutmeg
7	cups tart baking apples, peeled and sliced
1½	T butter or margarine

PREPARATION:

(a) Line pie dish with pastry, and sprinkle bottom with 2 T of the sugar. This helps to make the bottom crust flakier.

(b) Mix sugar, cinnamon and nutmeg and toss lightly through sliced apples.

(c) Heap apples into pastry-lined pie dish, and dot with butter.

(d) Cover with top crust which has slits cut in it. Seal and flute.

(e) Bake 50 - 60 minutes at 425 degrees, until crust is nicely browned and apples are cooked through (test with a toothpick).

Apple Crisp

If you don't have your own apple trees, you might enjoy a trip to a U-Pick Farm during Indian Summer. Seeing the bushel baskets full of harvest apples, the heaps of "jack-o-lanterns-to-be", and other fresh picked field foods gives you warm feeling that there is still order in the world.

INGREDIENTS: *Serves 4 - 6*

5	baking apples, peeled and sliced
2/3	cup brown sugar
1/2	cup old-fashioned oats
1/2	cup unbleached white flour
1	t cinnamon
1	t nutmeg
1/3	cup butter or margarine, softened

PREPARATION:

(a) Place apple slices in an 8″ square baking dish.

(b) Blend all other ingredients until crumbly, then spread over apples.

(c) Bake for 30 to 35 minutes in a 375 degree oven, until golden brown and apples are very tender.

Oregon Blueberry Crisp

If your freezer abounds with beautiful Oregon blueberries, a delicious alternative to apple crisp is blueberry crisp. To make, use the same topping and general directions.

NOTE: Freeze blueberries dry (without washing), then just rinse them in a strainer while still frozen and place directly into the baking dish.

Pumpkin Cupcakes

This pumpkin dessert is one of autumn's glories. Spices and raisins flavor these cupcakes that kids go for anytime, all the time — and so do adults!

INGREDIENTS: *Makes 24 - 30 cupcakes*

3	eggs		2¼	cups sugar
¾	cup vegetable oil		1½	t baking soda
1	pound can pumpkin		¾	t nutmeg
½	cup water		¾	t cinnamon
2½	cups unbleached white flour		1	cup raisins

4	ounces cream cheese, softened
3	T butter or margarine, softened
1	t vanilla
1	pound box powdered sugar
	chopped nuts, optional

PREPARATION:

(a)   Blend with mixer the eggs, oil, pumpkin and water.

(b)   Add flour, sugar, baking soda, nutmeg, cinnamon and raisins.

(c)   Pour into cupcake holders and bake at 350 degrees for 15 - 18 minutes. Cool.

(d)   Beat cream cheese, butter, vanilla and powdered sugar for frosting. Sprinkle with chopped nuts, if desired.

Pineapple Carrot Cake

You can make this a specialty by preparing it with chunks of pineapple, big nut pieces, and dates, so every bite becomes a sweet mouthful.

INGREDIENTS: *Makes a 9" x 13" cake*

1½	cups vegetable oil		1½	t cinnamon
3	eggs		1	cup carrots, shredded
2	cups brown sugar		1	cup unsweetened pineapple
1	t vanilla			chunks, drained
2½	cups unbleached white flour		1	cup dates, pitted and cut up
2	t baking soda		1	cup large walnut pieces

PREPARATION:

(a)   Blend together oil, eggs, brown sugar and vanilla.

(b)   Mix together dry ingredients and then add to blended wet ingredients; mix well.

(c)   Add carrots, pineapple, dates and walnuts; mix until well distributed.

(d)   Bake in a greased 9" x 13" pan for 45 to 50 minutes at 350 degrees.

This cake is very moist and delicious as is, but if you wish to have a topping, this one is perfect on it.

1	cup sugar
½	cup buttermilk
1	t baking soda
½	cup butter or margarine

Place all ingredients in a large saucepan and boil for 2 - 3 minutes, then pour over hot cake.

Lush Fruit and Chocolate Fondue

The popularity of this dessert is no mystery. It combines the rich, pure taste that chocolate lovers crave with the cool freshness of beautifully ripened fruit. It's a dessert that makes the search for the biggest and juiciest strawberries and cherries pay off.

INGREDIENTS: *Serves 6 - 8*

4	ounces unsweetened chocolate
1½	T butter or margarine
½	cup milk
1	cup honey
1	t vanilla

Variety of fresh strawberries, cherries, grapes, slices of bananas, pears and apples

PREPARATION:

(a)   Melt chocolate and butter in a saucepan over low heat, (or melt in microwave and then transfer to saucepan for remainder of preparation).

(b)   Gradually add milk and stir until well blended.

(c)   Add honey; stir and boil the mixture until it begins to thicken. Do not overcook.

(d)   Remove from heat and add vanilla. Pour into fondue pot and serve with attractively arranged fresh fruits.

NOTE: Fondue stores well in refrigerator. It is also delicious as an ice cream topping.

Cool Raspberry Fondue

This fun-to-eat dessert is refreshing on a sultry summer day. Enjoy it when raspberry picking is at its peak.

INGREDIENTS: *Serves 4 - 6*

1	pint fresh raspberries
1½	T cornstarch
1	T sugar
1	t lemon juice

Variety of fresh strawberries, cherries, grapes, slices of bananas, pears and apples.

PREPARATION:

(a)   Puree raspberries.

(b)   Combine berries, cornstarch and sugar in saucepan.

(c)   Cook and stir until thick and clear. Add lemon juice.

(d)   Pour into fondue pot and serve either warm or cool with attractively arranged fresh fruits.

NOTE: One 10 ounce package of frozen raspberries may be used when fresh raspberries are not available.

Peanut Butter Carob Bars

By the time school bells ring in the Fall, you'll be looking for ideas for wholesome lunch-box tuck-ins. These no-bake bars are a favorite with the cook because they are so easy, and with kids because they are so good.

INGREDIENTS: *Makes 36 bars*

½	cup butter or margarine
1	cup old-fashioned peanut butter
12	ounces carob chips
1	cup untoasted wheat germ
1	cup flaked coconut
1	cup unsalted peanuts
½	cup unsalted sunflower seeds

PREPARATION:

(a) Melt the butter, peanut butter and carob chips. (Can be done in microwave)

(b) Mix in other ingredients and pour into a 9″ x 13″ buttered dish.

(c) Refrigerate until firm, then cut into bars.

Cowboy Cookies

At the Brown's house there are always cowboy cookies smiling from inside the cookie jar. Thanks, Sue, for sharing this super recipe!

INGREDIENTS: *Makes 24 - 30 cookies*

1	cup, plus 2 T vegetable oil
1	cup brown sugar
1	cup granulated sugar
2	eggs
1	t vanilla
2	cups unbleached white flour
1	t salt
1	t baking soda
½	t baking powder
2	cups old-fashioned oats
½-1	cup chopped nuts
1-1½	cups chocolate chips

PREPARATION:

(a)   In a large bowl mix together the oil, sugars, eggs and vanilla.

(b)   Add all other ingredients and mix only until blended. Dough will be stiff.

(c)   Bake in 350 degree oven for 12 - 14 minutes. For best texture do not overbake.

Grandma's Oatmeal-Raisin Cookies

These soft-chewy cookies bring light-hearted memories to Jody of her mother's kitchen where something was usually baking. These cookies beg to be put into kids' hands or pockets, and are an absolute family favorite.

INGREDIENTS: *Makes 24 large cookies*

1	cup vegetable shortening		½	t salt
1	cup raisins		1	t cinnamon
½	cup water		½	t nutmeg
2	t vanilla		3	cups old-fashioned oats
1½	cups unbleached white flour		2	cups brown sugar
1	t baking soda		½	cup walnuts, chopped (optional)

PREPARATION:

(a) In a saucepan combine shortening, raisins and water. Bring to a boil and then cool; add vanilla.

(b) In a large bowl mix the flour, soda, salt, cinnamon, nutmeg, oats and brown sugar. Add cooled raisin mixture and stir well.

(c) Roll into round balls and do not flatten. Put on lightly greased baking sheet about 2″ apart and bake at 350 degrees 12 - 15 minutes. Do not overbake as they are best when very chewy.

Peanut Butter Bars

This sunshine bar warms you with kindness even at 10 degrees below!

INGREDIENTS: *Makes 12 bars*

½	cup vegetable shortening
½	cup brown sugar
½	cup granulated sugar
⅓	cup old-fashioned peanut butter
½	t vanilla
1	egg
¼	cup milk
1	cup unbleached white flour
½	t baking soda
1	cup old-fashioned rolled oats

PREPARATION:

(a)   Cream together shortening, sugars, peanut butter and vanilla until fluffy.

(b)   Add egg and milk; beat well.

(c)   Mix in the flour and baking soda, beating just until well combined. Stir in rolled oats.

(d)   Spread evenly in greased 9″ x 9″ pan. Bake at 350 degrees for 20 - 25 minutes.

(e)   If you desire, you can frost with your favorite chocolate or peanut butter icing.

Joe Froggers

Legend has it that in the 18th century old Uncle Joe would make these spicy molasses ginger cookies for the sailors. He lived next to a frog pond dotted with lily pads. The flat round shape of the cookies is reminiscent of the lily pads on which the frogs sat — thus the name Joe Froggers.

INGREDIENTS: *Makes 1½ dozen large cookies*

2	cups unbleached white flour		1	cup unsulphured molasses
1½	cups whole wheat flour		1	t baking soda
1	t salt		½	cup shortening
1½	t ginger		1	cup brown sugar
1	t cloves		½	cup water
½	t nutmeg		1	T vanilla
¼	t allspice			

PREPARATION:

(a) Blend together the flours, salt, ginger, cloves, nutmeg and allspice; set aside.

(b) Combine molasses and baking soda and set aside.

(c) Cream shortening and sugar, then add dry ingredients and mix well. To this add the molasses-baking soda mixture, water and vanilla; mix until well blended.

(d) Chill the dough for several hours or overnight.

(e) Roll dough on a floured surface ¼ inch thick. Cut with a 3″ or 4″ cookie cutter and bake on greased cookie sheets for 10 to 12 minutes at 375 degrees. To insure soft, moist cookies be sure that you do not overbake.

Peanut Butter Oatmeal Cookies

This recipe is the result of an over-the-phone collaberation between Jody and her friend, Sue Brown. The next time you have a craving for a cookie, sample these — you're sure to like them.

INGREDIENTS: *Makes about 24 large cookies*

2/3	cup butter or margarine
1/3	cup old-fashioned peanut butter
1	cup brown sugar
1/2	cup granulated sugar
1	large egg
1/4	cup milk
1	t vanilla
1	cup unbleached white flour
3	cups old-fashioned oats
1/2	t salt
1	t baking soda
1/2	t baking powder
1	cup walnuts, chopped (optional)

PREPARATION:

(a) Cream together the butter, peanut butter, and sugars.

(b) Blend and mix in the egg, milk, and vanilla.

(c) In another bowl stir together the flour, oats, salt, baking soda and baking powder. Mix into other ingredients.

(d) Drop by rounded tablespoonsful onto a lightly greased baking sheet. Bake at 350 degrees about 13 minutes. Do not overbake.

Tapioca Pudding

This recipe is used today almost entirely by homemakers who learned to like it at their grand-mother's tables. It's good-tasting, easy to make and inexpensive.

INGREDIENTS: *Makes 5 half-cup servings*

3	T tapioca
2½	T sugar
2	cups milk
1	egg, separated
2	T sugar
1	t vanilla

PREPARATION:

(a)   Mix tapioca, 2½ T sugar, milk and egg yolk in double boiler; let stand.

(b)   Beat egg white until foamy; then add 2 T sugar, beating until soft peaks form. Set this aside.

(c)   Cook tapioca mixture over high heat, stirring constantly about 6 - 8 minutes, until desired consistency.

(d)   Gradually add the beaten egg white, folding carefully, only until blended. (Do not overstir as pudding will become too thin.) Blend in vanilla. Cool 20 minutes.

(e)   Stir. Pour into dessert dishes or serving bowl. Serve warm or chilled.

Microwave Egg Custard

This is a wonderful "on the spot" dessert or after-school snack.

INGREDIENTS: *Serves 6 - 8*

6	eggs
1/2	cup sugar
3 1/2	cups milk
2	t vanilla

PREPARATION:

(a)   Place individual custard dishes (1/2 cup size) into a glass baking dish.

(b)   Beat the eggs and sugar together until thick and foamy.

(c)   Add the milk and vanilla and beat until well mixed.

(d)   Pour into custard dishes. Cook in microwave about 10 - 12 minutes. Turn dishes every 2 minutes.

(e)   Custard is done when barely set and moist looking in the center. It will cook some during the cooling period. Chill and serve with nutmeg, cinnamon or fresh fruit if desired.

Microwave Pumpkin Custard

Rich with maple syrup, eggs, and pumpkin, this dessert makes a delightful ending to a Fall dinner when making a quick dessert seems a necessity.

INGREDIENTS: *Serves 4*

2	eggs
¼	cup pure maple syrup
¾	cup canned pumpkin
½	t cinnamon
¼	t ground nutmeg
¼	t ground ginger
1	5 ounce can evaporated milk
	whipped cream (optional)
	chopped nuts (optional)

PREPARATION:

(a) Beat eggs slightly, add maple syrup, pumpkin, cinnamon, nutmeg, ginger and evaporated milk. Beat until blended.

(b) Fill four custard cups (6 ounce each) with custard.

(c) Cook uncovered 4 - 4½ minutes or until set. Stir each cup four times during cooking and reposition cups for more even cooking.

(d) Chill and add toppings, if desired.

Brown Rice Pudding

This is an old-time favorite that is still as popular as in pioneer days. It's a great warm-from-the-oven dessert.

INGREDIENTS: *Serves 6 - 8*

2	cups short-grain brown rice, cooked		½	t grated lemon rind
3	eggs		3¼	cups milk
¼	cup honey		1	t nutmeg
2	t vanilla		2	T butter or margarine
½	cup raisins			

PREPARATION:

(a) Break eggs into a deep two-quart casserole; beat slightly with fork. Stir in honey, vanilla, raisins and lemon rind.

(b) Add milk to cooked rice and stir into egg mixture.

(c) Sprinkle on nutmeg; then dot with small pieces of butter.

(d) Set casserole into a large baking pan and fill pan with hot water.

(e) Bake at 300 degrees for 1 hour and 25 minutes, stirring once after ½ hour of baking. (To avoid breaking top, insert spoon at end of pudding; draw gently.) When done a knife inserted in center comes out clean.

(f) Remove casserole from baking pan and cool. Serve slightly warm or cold, topped with whipped cream.

Company Desserts

"Occasionally there are times when we enjoy serving sweet and tempting desserts to our guests. In the Company Desserts section are recipes that feature that all-time favorite flavor — chocolate, plus warm fruit desserts, pies, cakes and other special treats laced with liqueurs."

Jody and Elsie

Happy Endings
Company Desserts

Mile High Pie

When daffodils and robins announce the arrival of Spring, and strawberries are again appearing in the market, it's time to bring a refreshing taste of Spring to your dinner table.

Oregon strawberries are beauties that taste as good as they look. If you have lived in other areas of the country, as we have, you undoubtedly appreciate the huge, luscious berries so abundant from our local strawberry farms. This high pie has an unusual, delicate, fluffy filling. Thanks to Sue Malen of Boise, Idaho for sharing this recipe.

INGREDIENTS: *Makes one 10" pie*

No-roll crust:

1½	cups unbleached white flour		2	T milk
1	t sugar		½	cup vegetable oil
1	t salt			

Filling:

2	egg whites, beaten until fluffy		1	T lemon juice
1	pint frozen strawberries, partially thawed		½	pint whipping cream, whipped
½	cup sugar			

PREPARATION:

(a)   Prepare crust by mixing all ingredients directly in a 10" pie dish. Pat dough to fit dish. Bake 10 minutes at 425 degrees and cool.

(b)   For the filling, beat egg whites and when fluffy add berries, sugar and lemon juice. Beat at very high speed for about 10 minutes.

(c)   Gently fold in whipped cream. Pour into cooled crust and freeze 6 - 8 hours. Serve frozen.

Fresh Strawberry Pie

A no-bake pie; cool to make in summer. It's a real show-off dessert made with little effort.

INGREDIENTS: *Makes one 8″ pie*

Pastry for 8″ pie shell

1	quart fresh strawberries
¾	cup sugar
3	T cornstarch
	whipped cream or ice cream (optional)

PREPARATION:

(a)   Make a standard recipe for an 8″ pie shell. Bake and cool.

(b)   Divide berries in half. Line pie shell with half of the fresh, uncooked berries.

(c)   Crush remaining half of berries and mix with sugar and cornstarch in a saucepan. Cook until thick. Cool, then pour over fresh berries in shell. Chill.

(d)   Serve topped with whipped cream or ice cream, if desired.

Blueberry Rum Pie

This blueberry cheesecake dessert is colorful and tempting, with a luscious flavor blend.

INGREDIENTS: *Makes one 9" pie*

Crust:
1	cup graham cracker crumbs
2	T untoasted wheat germ

2	T unprocessed bran
1/4	cup vegetable oil

Filling:
4	3 ounce packages cream cheese, softened
1/2	cup honey
2	eggs, well beaten

1/4	t rum extract
2	cups fresh blueberries, rinsed and drained

Topping:
1	cup sour cream
1	t honey
1	t vanilla

PREPARATION:

(a) Mix graham cracker crumbs, wheat germ, bran, oil and honey; then press into bottom of a 9" pie dish. Refrigerate while continuing with the next steps.

(b) Beat cream cheese until fluffy. Gradually beat in honey, then eggs and rum extract.

(c) Fold in blueberries, then pour mixture into prepared crust.

(d) Bake at 375 degrees for 25 minutes or until filling is set. Remove from oven and cool for at least 30 minutes.

(e) In a small bowl mix remaining ingredients and pour evenly over pie. Bake at 400 degrees for 5 minutes, no more. Garnish with additional fresh blueberries. Chill.

Walnut Chess Pie

Elsie's company special. It never fails to please her guests.

INGREDIENTS: *Makes one 9" pie*

Pastry for one single crust 9" pie

1½	cups brown sugar
1	T unbleached white flour
2	eggs
3	T milk
1½	t vanilla
½	cup butter or margarine, melted
1½	cups large walnut pieces

PREPARATION:

(a)   Mix brown sugar and flour.

(b)   Beat in thoroughly the eggs, milk, vanilla and butter.

(c)   Fold in walnuts.

(d)   Pour into pastry-lined pie dish.

(e)   Bake 40 - 50 minutes at 375 degrees, just until filling is set and nicely browned.

Pecan-Glazed Pumpkin Pie

Baking this pie brings back childhood memories to Elsie of the drives past old country places as her family drove from New York State into Pennsylvania for the Thanksgiving feast.

INGREDIENTS: *Makes two 9″ pies*

Pastry for 2 one-crust pies

1	29 ounce can pumpkin		1	t nutmeg
2	cups brown sugar		6	eggs, beaten
1	t (slightly rounded) cinnamon		1	cup milk
1	t ginger			

PREPARATION:

(a)   In a large bowl beat together all ingredients.

(b)   Pour into pastry-lined pie dish. To prevent edge of crust from over-browning cover edges with a 3-4″ strip of foil

(c)   Bake 45 to 55 minutes at 375 degrees, just until a knife inserted in filling comes out clean.

Pecan Glaze

3   T butter or margarine, melted
2/3   cup brown sugar
2/3   cup pecans, coarsely chopped

Combine butter, sugar and pecans. Spread gently over cooled pie to cover top. Broil 5″ below heat until mixture begins to bubble, about three minutes. Watch carefully.

Chocolate Marble Cheesecake

This recipe originated in Switzerland. The chocolate and creamy cheese blend superbly in this velvet smooth chocolate cheese dessert. It's definitely a special occasion dessert. Plan to make it at least 12 hours before you serve it for perfect texture and flavor.

INGREDIENTS: *Makes a 9½" cheesecake*

Crust:
1	cup graham cracker crumbs	¼	cup vegetable oil
2	T untoasted wheat germ	2	T honey
2	T unprocessed bran		

Filling:
3	8 ounce packages Neufchatel cream cheese, softened	1½	cups sour cream
¾	cup honey	2	t honey
¾	t vanilla	½	t vanilla
3	eggs, well beaten	¼	cup chocolate syrup (or chocolate fondue)
½	cup chocolate syrup or chocolate fondue (recipe on page 128)		

PREPARATION:

(a) Mix graham cracker crumbs, wheat germ, bran, oil and honey; then press into bottom of a 9½" springform pan. Refrigerate while continuing with the next steps.

(b) In a mixing bowl blend together the cheese, honey, vanilla and eggs. Blend until the mixture is smooth and creamy.

(c) In a small bowl mix sour cream, honey and vanilla. Refrigerate to use later.

(d) Pour half of the cream cheese mixture into the prepared crust. Drizzle the ½ cup of chocolate syrup over the mixture, then cover with the other half of the cream cheese mixture. With a thin knife or fondue fork cut through the batter to marbleize it.

Chocolate Marble Cheesecake

(e)   Bake at 325 degrees for 30 - 40 minutes, until center is set. Cool, but do not refrigerate.

(f)   Pour sour cream mixture over baked cheesecake. Drizzle remaining chocolate syrup over top and marbleize. Bake at 450 degrees for 5 minutes, no more. Cool and refrigerate overnight or at least 12 hours.

Layered Raspberry Tart

Race with the birds to see who will get the juiciest, ripest berries so you can enjoy this fresh raspberry tart. It amply rewards anyone who makes it or eats it.

INGREDIENTS: *Makes one 9½" tart*

Crust:
1	cup unbleached white flour		$\frac{1}{3}$	cup vegetable oil
1	T sugar		1	egg yolk
$\frac{1}{2}$	t salt		$\frac{1}{2}$	t vanilla

Cream cheese layer:
1	8 ounce package Neufchatel, cream cheese, softened		2	t honey
			1	t vanilla

Raspberry layer:
3	cups raspberries, fresh or frozen		$\frac{2}{3}$	cup water
1	cup sugar		3	T cornstarch

PREPARATION:

(a)   In a medium-sized bowl blend the flour, sugar and salt. With a table knife mix in the oil, egg yolk and vanilla until well blended. Press into the bottom of a 9½" tart pan (or spring-form pan) making a slightly higher edge. Bake at 400 degrees for 7 to 10 minutes, until lightly browned. Cool.

(b)   Mix softened cream cheese, honey and vanilla until creamy and smooth. When baked pastry is slightly cooled spread this mixture to within ⅛" of the edge.

(c)   Distribute 2 cups of the raspberries over the cream cheese layer.

(d)   In a saucepan mix 1 cup crushed raspberries, sugar and water. Bring quickly to a boil, then lower heat to simmer. In the meantime mix the cornstarch with enough additional water to make a thin paste. Stir into the simmering berries and continue cooking just until thickened and clear. Cool 10 - 15 minutes. Pour over the berries and chill completely before serving.

Chocolate Mousse Pie

After an evening patio meal, delight your guests with this delicately-flavored rum chocolate pie. It's a show-off dessert that's as good as it looks.

INGREDIENTS: *Makes one 10″ pie*

1⅓	cups fine chocolate wafer crumbs (about 18 wafers)		
3	T butter or margarine, softened		
⅓	cup sugar	3	T heavy cream
4	T rum (or 3½ T water & ¼ T rum extract)	3	egg whites
1	12 ounce package semisweet chocolate chips	1½	cups whipping cream, whipped

PREPARATION:

(a)   Mix chocolate wafer crumbs and butter until crumbly. Press on bottom and sides of a 10″ pie plate. Bake at 375 degrees for 8 minutes. Cool.

(b)   In a small saucepan mix together sugar and rum. Cook over low heat just until sugar is dissolved.

(c)   In a double boiler melt the chocolate, then stir in the 3 T heavy cream. Add to this the sugar and rum mixture. Cool.

(d)   Beat egg whites until they are stiff and stand in peaks, then fold into the cooled chocolate mixture.

(e)   Gently fold the whipped cream into the above and spoon into the cooled pie shell. Chill several hours before serving.

(f)   Garnish with additional whipped cream or chocolate curls.

Chocolate Lover's Delight

This dessert is almost like magic! Preparation is "quick as a wink", and the resulting velvety-smooth richness is hard to surpass. For an elegant presentation serve in stemmed glassware.

INGREDIENTS: *Serves 6 - 8*

1	12 ounce package semi-sweet chocolate chips
1¼	cups scalded milk
2	eggs

whipped cream for topping (optional)

PREPARATION:

(a)   Put chocolate chips in blender. Slowly add hot milk through the top hole in blender lid. Blend until chocolate is melted. Add eggs and blend thoroughly.

(b)   Pour into serving dishes and chill.

NOTE: Because this is a very rich dessert, make serving portions about half a cup.

Pumpkin Cream Royale

This elegant no-bake dessert has the appearance of a cheesecake and the texture of a mousse. The whipped cream piping and slices of almonds create an eye-pleasing dessert you'd be proud to serve. Try it for your next Fall holiday buffet.

INGREDIENTS: *Serves 10 - 12*

Crust:
1	cup graham cracker crumbs
2	T untoasted wheat germ
2	T unprocessed bran

1/4	cup vegetable oil
2	T honey

Filling:
8	ounces cream cheese, softened
1 1/4	cups sugar
1/2	t ground ginger
1	t cinnamon
1/4	t cloves
1/2	t salt

1	29 ounce can pumpkin
2	envelopes unflavored gelatin
1/4	cup cold water
2	cups whipping cream, whipped
1/2	cup slivered almonds, toasted

PREPARATION:

(a) Combine cracker crumbs, wheat germ and bran. Add the oil and honey. Press firmly into a 9″ springform pan.

(b) Blend cream cheese, sugar, spices and salt.

(c) Add pumpkin and continue beating until well blended.

(d) In a small saucepan, sprinkle gelatin over water. Place over low heat and stir until gelatin is dissolved. Stir into pumpkin mixture.

(e) Fold in whipped cream. Pour mixture over crust.

(f) Chill overnight. Remove sides from pan. Garnish sides and top of dessert with whipped cream piping and slivered almonds.

German Apple Strudel

This old-world favorite becomes easy to prepare with this flaky sour cream pastry. Jody's sister-in-law, Linda Rosenberg, from Omaha served this to her on her first Christmas as a new bride. It has now become a family tradition for holidays at their house, too.

INGREDIENTS: *Makes 3 strudel*

¼	pound butter		1½	cups raisins
¼	pound margarine		1	cup sugar
1	cup sour cream		1	cup walnuts, chopped
2	cups unbleached white flour		6	T cinnamon
6	large tart apples, peeled and coarsely chopped		¾	cup flaked coconut

PREPARATION:

(a)　Cream the butter, margarine and sour cream together. Then add the two cups of flour and knead like pie crust.

(b)　Wrap dough and refrigerate for several hours.

(c)　Divide dough into three balls. Refrigerate balls not being rolled out. Roll out each ball into a paper-thin 12″ x 14″ rectangle.

(d)　Mix raisins, sugar, walnuts, cinnamon and coconut together — use ⅓ of this mixture for each strudel. Place ⅓ of the chopped apples 4″ from the edge all along one side. Sprinkle ⅓ of the sugar mixture over apples.

(e)　Gently fold the dough over the filling and slowly and evenly roll into a tight roll. Seal ends. If you are going to bake it at this point, place on a lightly greased jelly roll pan and curve slightly to form a crescent. If you want to freeze it, roll it onto waxed paper and seal tight. (Can be baked frozen at 400 degrees for 40 to 50 minutes.)

German Apple Strudel

(f)   Repeat with other dough.

(g)   Bake at 375 degrees 40 - 50 minutes, or until lightly browned. Remove from pan. Cool or serve slightly warm, topped with ice cream.

German Chocolate Cake

This moist cake with old-fashioned flavor is one of the tastiest cakes we've ever had the privilege to eat. It is picture pretty and a perfect melt-in-your-mouth dessert.

INGREDIENTS: *Makes a three-layer cake*

4	ounces German sweet chocolate	1½	t vanilla
½	cup boiling water	2¼	cups unbleached white flour
1	cup butter or margarine	1	t baking soda
2	cups sugar	1	cup buttermilk (fresh or powdered)
4	egg yolks	4	egg whites, stiffly beaten

PREPARATION:

(a) Melt chocolate in boiling water and cool.

(b) Cream butter with sugar until fluffy.

(c) Add yolks, one at a time, beating well after each. Then blend in vanilla and chocolate.

(d) Sift flour with soda and add alternately with buttermilk to chocolate mixture, beating after each addition, until smooth. Gently fold in beaten egg whites.

(e) Pour into three greased 9″ layer pans, lined on bottoms with waxed paper. Bake at 350 degrees for 30 - 35 minutes. Cool.

Coconut-Walnut Frosting: *Makes about 3 cups*

Combine:	1¼ cups evaporated milk	½	cup butter or margarine
	1 cup sugar	1½ t vanilla	
	3 slightly beaten egg yolks		

Cook and stir over medium heat until thickened — about 12 minutes.

Add: 1½ cups flaked coconut   1½ cups walnuts, chopped

Cook until thick enough to spread, beating occasionally.

Classic Carrot Cake

Some weekend when you're looking for an idea for a unique outing, try a thunderegg dig in Central Oregon. With a pick and shovel you can dig into volcanic soil deposited millions of years ago, in search of the agate-filled balls that are now the state rock of Oregon.

Be sure to pack a picnic to enjoy in the wide-open spaces. A great ending to your picnic would be this all-time favorite moist cake.

INGREDIENTS: *Makes one 13" x 9" cake or three 8" layers*

1½	cups unbleached white flour	1½	cups vegetable oil
½	cup whole wheat flour	4	eggs
1	t baking soda	3	cups finely grated carrots
1	t baking powder	1	cup crushed pineapple, drained
1	t cinnamon	½	cup raisins
2	cups sugar	½	cup large walnut pieces

PREPARATION:

(a)   Mix the dry ingredients together; add the oil and blend.

(b)   Add the eggs one at a time and beat after each addition.

(c)   Add the carrots, pineapple, raisins, and walnuts and blend well.

(d)   Pour into lightly greased pan and bake at 350 degrees for 1 hour if in the 13" x 9" pan and bake for 30 minutes if using the 8" layer pans.

TOPPING:

1	8 ounce package cream cheese, softened	2	t vanilla
2	cups powdered sugar	½	cup walnuts, finely chopped
½	cup butter or margarine, softened		

Blend cream cheese, sugar, butter and vanilla. Spread evenly over cake and sprinkle with chopped nuts.

Hot Fudge Sundae Cake

This dessert is delightfully simple, and appealing to the eye as well as to the palate. You need only one dish for mixing and baking, so clean up is a breeze.

INGREDIENTS: *Serves 6 - 8*

1	cup unbleached white flour
¾	cup granulated sugar (or ½ cup honey)
2	T cocoa
2	t baking powder
½	cup milk
2	T vegetable oil
1	t vanilla
1	cup walnuts, chopped
1	cup brown sugar
¼	cup cocoa
1¾	cups very hot tap water

PREPARATION:

(a)   In ungreased 9″ x 9″ baking dish stir together flour, sugar, cocoa and baking powder.

(b)   Add milk, oil and vanilla, stirring with a fork until smooth. Blend in nuts.

(c)   Spread mixture evenly in baking dish, then sprinkle with brown sugar and cocoa.

(d)   Pour hot water over the entire dish, then bake for 40 minutes at 350 degrees.

(e)   Let stand for at least 15 minutes before serving. Spoon into stemmed dessert dishes. Top with vanilla ice cream and spoon sauce over each serving.

Cowboy Sheet Cake

Outdoor parties are the great American pastime. Next time friends and neighbors gather and you offer to bring dessert, try this time-tested recipe with chocolate-y, melt-in-your-mouth goodness.

INGREDIENTS: *Makes 24 servings or 48 party sized squares*

2	cups unbleached white flour		3	T cocoa
2	cups sugar		2	eggs, well beaten
1/4	t salt		1	t baking soda
1	cup butter or margarine		1/2	cup buttermilk (fresh or powdered)
1	cup water		1	t vanilla

PREPARATION:

(a)   Sift flour, measure, and resift with sugar and salt.

(b)   In a saucepan put butter, water, and cocoa. Bring to a boil and pour over flour and sugar mixture.

(c)   In another bowl put eggs, soda, buttermilk and vanilla. Add to above mixture and mix well.

(d)   Bake in a greased and floured shallow cake pan (15 1/2 x 10 1/2 x 1). Bake for 20 minutes at 350 degrees.

(e)   Start icing the last 5 minutes cake is baking.

CHOCOLATE ICING:

1/2	cup butter or margarine		3 1/2	cups powdered sugar, sifted
3	T cocoa		1	t vanilla
6	T milk		1/2	cup walnuts, chopped

Mix butter, cocoa and milk in saucepan. Heat over low heat; do not boil. Remove from heat and add powdered sugar and vanilla. Mix well. Frost cake as soon as it is removed from the oven. Sprinkle frosted cake with chopped walnuts.

Grand Marnier Chocolate Dipped Strawberries

Planning a special summer outdoor party? This dessert is a real conversation piece and is well worth your time and effort.

INGREDIENTS: *Serves 4 - 6*

1	quart fresh ripe strawberries, rinsed and patted dry
	Grand Marnier liqueur
¾	cup semi-sweet chocolate chips
1	T vegetable oil

PREPARATION:

(a)   With a flavor injector or syringe inject each berry with desired amount of Grand Marnier.

(b)   Be sure berries are completely dry before dipping.

(c)   Heat chocolate chips and oil together until melted and smooth. (This can be done in the microwave or over hot but not boiling water.) Keep warm.

(d)   Insert skewer or pick in stem end of strawberry. Dip tapered end of strawberry about one half of the way up to the stem in chocolate. Lift out quickly and twirl slightly over chocolate to let excess run off.

(e)   For perfectly dipped berries dry by standing skewers in a clean needle flower arranger or a piece of styrofoam.

(f)   Dipped berries can be refrigerated for several hours.

Strawberry Chantillys

These lacy, chocolate-covered meringues enchant people of all ages. Topping them with straw-berries and whipped cream makes this one of summer's best treats. Every forkful brings delight.

INGREDIENTS: *Serves 4*

3	egg whites	¼	t almond extract
½	t cream of tartar	1	cup sugar
1	t vanilla		
1	pint whipping cream, whipped	8	ounces semi-sweet chocolate chips
2	T powdered sugar	3	T hot water
2	T brandy (optional)	1	quart fresh strawberries

PREPARATION:

(a) Beat room-temperature egg whites with cream of tartar, vanilla and almond extract. Gradually add sugar.

(b) Cover baking sheet with baking parchment and divide meringue into 3″ circles, making 8 meringues. Spread evenly with knife or spatula. Bake in a 250 degree oven about 30 to 40 minutes. Remove from oven; cool, and set aside.

(c) For chocolate layer, melt and mix chocolate chips and 3 T hot water until smooth.

(d) To assemble, place one meringue layer on serving plate. Spread with chocolate, then whipped cream, then a layer of sliced strawberries. Repeat with second meringue in same manner. Place halved strawberries all around sides and top with one whole berry in the center with tip up.

NOTE: For serving 10 - 12 people, make three 8″ circle meringues, and assemble as with individual chantillys.

Banana Split Fantasy

Every forkful of this dessert brings delight! It's very easy to make and your guests are sure to want the recipe.

INGREDIENTS: *Makes a 13" x 9" dessert*

1	cup graham cracker crumbs
2	T untoasted wheat germ
2	T unprocessed bran

¼	cup vegetable oil
2	T honey

1	cup butter or margarine
2	cups powdered sugar
2	eggs
5	bananas, sliced
1	20 ounce can unsweetened crushed pineapple, drained

1	pint whipping cream, whipped and sweetened to taste
4	T low-sugar strawberry jam or jelly, softened in microwave or over low heat

PREPARATION:

(a) Blend graham cracker crumbs, wheat germ, bran, vegetable oil and honey. Press into a 12" x 9" baking pan.

(b) Beat together for 10 minutes the butter, powdered sugar, and eggs. Spread over graham cracker crust.

(c) Distribute the banana slices evenly over the above layers; then cover with drained pineapple.

(d) Cover entire dessert with whipped cream and drizzle softened strawberry jam or jelly over top.

Butter Pecan Turtle Bars

Christmas at the Palmers just wouldn't be the same without having these cookies among the assortment of party desserts.

INGREDIENTS: *Makes fifty 1¼″ squares*

Crust:
2   cups unbleached white flour
1   cup firmly packed brown sugar
½   cup butter or margarine, softened

Caramel layer:
1   cup pecan halves
⅔   cup butter or margarine
½   cup firmly packed brown sugar

Topping:
1   12 ounce package semi sweet chocolate chips

PREPARATION:

(a)   In a bowl combine crust ingredients. Mix at medium speed, scraping sides of bowl often, for 2 - 3 minutes, or until particles are fine. Pat firmly into an ungreased 13″ x 9″ pan.

(b)   Place pecans evenly over crust.

(c)   For caramel layer, combine brown sugar and butter and cook over medium heat, stirring constantly. Boil for one minute, then pour evenly over pecans and crust.

(d)   Bake on middle rack of oven for 18 - 22 minutes at 350 degrees. Caramel layer should be bubbly and crust should be light golden brown.

(e)   Immediately after removing from the oven sprinkle the chocolate chips evenly over the top. Allow the chocolate chips to melt for 2 - 3 minutes, then with a rubber spatula spread like icing. Cool, then cut into squares.

INDEX

ORDER FORM

Please send me _____ copies of **Eating the Oregon Way** at $8.95 per copy, plus $1.50 per copy to cover postage and handling.

Enclosed is my check for $_____ payable to:

Berry Patch Press
4 Camelot Court, Lake Oswego, Oregon 97034

NAME _____

ADDRESS _____

CITY _____ STATE_____ ZIP_____

ORDER FORM

Please send me _____ copies of **Eating the Oregon Way** at $8.95 per copy, plus $1.50 per copy to cover postage and handling.

Enclosed is my check for $_____ payable to:

Berry Patch Press
4 Camelot Court, Lake Oswego, Oregon 97034

NAME _____

ADDRESS _____

CITY _____ STATE_____ ZIP_____